Going the Distance: A Handbook for Faculty Who Teach Online

Second Edition
by Happy Gingras, Patricia Adams and Evelyn Beck

Order information:

To order copies of this book, please contact Part-Time Press, at P.O. Box 130117, Ann Arbor, Michigan 48113-0117, or email orders@Part-TimePress.com. The phone/fax number is 734-930-6854.

First Edition: April, 2008
Revised: December, 2016
Second Edition, 2019

Copyright 2019, *Part-Time Press, Inc.*

ISBN-13: 978-0-940017-51-1 (paperback)

Printed in the United States of America.

Introduction

How many times have you turned to YouTube for an instructional video to learn to complete a home-improvement task? How often have you used online tutorial videos and discussion forums to solve a computer problem? If you are an average American, the answer to these and other distance education questions is...frequently (and maybe even daily).

Distance education in the United States can be traced back to correspondence courses and then to instructional television. Now, though, distance education is used globally in primary, secondary, and higher education as well as in industry, by non-profits seeking to educate the public and even in political campaigns. A world-wide embrace of online learning has shifted the educational landscape.

To give you an idea of what this digital revolution looks like in higher education, let's look at some numbers. According to the National Center for Education Statistics, there are currently approximately 20 million students enrolled at American colleges and universities, up from 15 million in 2000. Of those, approximately 6.3 million students enroll in online courses. The Babson Survey Research Group reports that 2019 marks the 14th consecutive year online course enrollment has increased at American educational institutions. Additionally, between 2012 and 2016, the Babson survey reports that the number of students studying strictly on campus dropped by over one million.

Why do so many students choose online courses? Flexibility. Students enrolling in online courses are afforded flexibility of location, schedule, and pacing. Students can take courses anywhere in the world, though the Babson report acknowledges that 85 percent of students taking online courses are doing so at a college within their home state. The availability of online courses worldwide, however, allows students to broaden their choices of schools and consider options that were not available even as recently as a decade ago.

Flexibility of scheduling is another benefit of online learning. Busy students with many responsibilities can complete their course-work after their work day is done. Students needing to take courses toward a degree are no longer restricted to on-campus course schedules. Students can enroll in courses they may not otherwise have been able to take, because the class sessions were held on campus during times that were not convenient for those students.

Finally, flexibility of pacing allows students to work toward degrees at their own pace. For example, online students routinely examine all coursework on the first day of class. This allows them to complete course work well before scheduled deadlines. Students tend to appreciate this opportunity, as it allows them to complete assignments before attacking papers, projects and exams in on campus courses. Part-time students routinely use online course availability to choose how many courses they want to complete in a semester without having to worry when courses are scheduled on campus.

Not everything about distance education has been positive, though. Online courses and degree programs have historically had lower retention rates (numbers of students finishing courses or degrees) than their traditional face-to-face counterparts. For example, a study in the journal *Online Learning* (James et. al. 2015) reported a lower retention rate for students taking only online courses than for those who mixed their online learning with face-to-face learning in traditional or blended courses. When you ask instructors who teach both online and face-to-face, you are likely to hear that their online students "disappear" more frequently than their face-to-face students.

However, the same study from *Online Learning* acknowledged that much of the attrition in online courses is unrelated to course content and was usually related to extraneous circumstances. A report from *Campus Technology* in 2018 (Carter) reported that students taking at least some of their courses online finished their degrees more often and faster than students taking only face-to-face courses. One thing is truly clear in the world of education, online learning is an integral part of higher education and this is not likely to change in the near future.

The availability of improved technology has revolutionized the delivery of distance education. What was once thought of as a less effective means of learning can now be even more engaging and enriching than a face-to-face course with the effective use of tech tools. This same technology can enhance face-to-face courses, and create hybrid or blended education in which in-class learning is enhance by online assignments and resources.

In our book *Flipped and Blended Learning: A Comprehensive Guide* (Adams & Gingras, 2018), we outline how to use technology to enhance the face-to-face experience. Flipping a classroom, by providing online lectures, learning activities and resources, and in-class active learning, is one of the best things to develop from improved technology in our opinions. Even better news, though, is that with current technologies you can create an online version or alternative to nearly anything that can be done face-to-face. The possibilities are endless!

We have seen the demand for educational technology grow with the expansion of distance education. Higher education publishers are responding; the availability of online texts, labs, interactive learning activities and tools is growing. One specific area of growth worth mentioning is open educational resources. Open resources are those that are free to use by anyone, and are dependable and widely available. Thanks to the demand from educators, there are now free textbooks with the same high quality control as those we have historically used. Publishers have adapted their texts for less expensive online use and embedded valuable learning activities. There are countless online videos and case studies available. The lists of resources are growing every day, and many are available with copyrights that allow you to customize them or use only the portions that are relevant to you. Even more are created to be accessible to users with challenges, such as learning disabilities, vision issues, and other things that may hinder learning without consideration for their needs.

With such a huge array of resources available to the online educator today, teaching online can be an overwhelming prospect. Having choices is wonderful, until you have too many choices and too little knowledge about how to use them, right? The good news is that teaching an online course is about far more than assembling an organized and entertaining group of tech tools, and if you hope to teach an engaging course that students not only finish, but finish successfully, you'll need to work purposefully and plan your course meticulously.

Going the Distance: A Handbook for Faculty Who Teach Online provides faculty with the mentoring and support to be effective, successful distance educators. Whether you are teaching your first online course or looking for a way to improve the courses you already teach, this book will offer you a road map to improvement so that you can be the most successful online educator possible.

We know that you will both enjoy and find this book useful. We are confident you will end your time with us with more tools in your online teaching toolkit, and mastery of the skills necessary to venture into (new areas of) distance learning from a perspective of readiness.

Happy Gingras, Patricia Adams & Evelyn Beck

Table of Contents

Table of Figures

Chapter One

Getting Started

According to Inside Higher Ed's 2018 "Survey of Faculty Attitudes on Technology," the percentage of college instructors who are teaching online and blended courses is growing. In 2013, 30 percent of college faculty reported teaching online. In 2018, 44 percent of faculty taught online. Perhaps when you decided to teach college, you envisioned a classroom full of eager faces. Now, you're tackling a course in which your classroom is a computer screen and interactions are digital. Are you ready to facilitate online discussions, plan virtual field trips and lab assignments? Your job will be to make sure that your online courses achieve student outcomes comparable to those of face-to-face courses. We're here to help you do just that!

Consider a busy highway. You are the tour director on a bus full of tourists hanging on your every word as you drive down the road. They can see you, and you can see them, you can point out the sights around you, and no matter what happens you will end up at the same destination together.

Now imagine you are the same tour director, but you are in a car alone and your tourists are somewhere on the highway in their own cars. How can you show them the sights? How can you make sure they find the places they are meant to find, learn the things they are meant to learn and end their journey where it is meant to end?

This is the challenge of online learning, but it is also its biggest asset. With advances in technology, you can now simultaneously teach a student who is sitting in front of you with a laptop and one who is hundreds or thousands of miles away. The online classroom is full of obstacles, but also full of possibilities.

Whether this is your first online course or you've taught at a distance before, approach a new course as though it's your first. This book will provide you the roadmap necessary to complete your journey. However, as with teaching face-to-face, preparation is necessary. In a classroom, it's easy to recover from a teaching mishap or a planning error; in a distance learning situation, it's much more difficult.

Keep in mind these two major factors while preparing for your distance education courses: you must have comfortable command of the technology and you must not lose sight of the fact that the human touch of the teacher-student relationship is necessary for learning. Master the technology, but do not get so wrapped up in it that individual students are neglected! The keys to success are to keep the lines of communication open and always be well prepared.

1.1 Online Lingo 101

Important Distance Learning Terms

Accessibility: The degree to which a resource is usable by someone with physical or mental challenges or disabilities.

Analog : A signal that is received in the same form in which it is transmitted, while the amplitude and frequency may vary.

Amplitude: The amount of variety in a signal. Commonly thought of as the height of a wave.

American Standard Code for Information Interexchange (ASCII): A computer language used to convert letters, numbers, and control codes into a digital code understood by most computers.

Asynchronous: Communication in which interaction between parties does not take place simultaneously.

Asynchronous Transmission Mode (ATM): A method of sending data in irregular time intervals using a code such as ASCII. ATM allows most modern computers to communicate with one another easily.

Audio Bridge: A device used in audio conferencing that connects multiple telephone lines.

Audio Conferencing: Voice only connection of more than two sites using standard telephone lines.

Augmented Reality (AR): An interactive experience in the real-world environment in which the real-world objects or locations are augmented by a computer-based interactive experience.

Band: A range of frequencies between defined upper and lower limits.

Bandwidth: Information carrying capacity of a communication channel.

Binary: A computer language developed with only two letters in its alphabet.

Bit: Abbreviation for a single binary digit.

Blended Learning: Instructional approach that combines face-to-face learning with computer-based learning.

Blog: Short for weblog. An online journal viewed as a website that can be updated regularly with dated posts.

Breadcrumb Path (or Breadcrumb Trail): A graphics based control element that allows users to navigate on web pages.

Browser: Software that allows you to find and see information on the Internet.

Buffering: Occurs when videos or live feeds are attempted with limited network bandwidth or slow connections.

Byte: A single computer word, generally eight bits.

Central Processing Unit (CPU): The component of a computer in which data processing takes place.

Channel : The smallest subdivision of a circuit, usually with a path in only one direction.

Chat Room: Often called Online Chat or simply Chat. An online meeting room using web-based conferencing tools to allow users to interact by live voice and video feeds.

Codec (COder/DECoder): Device used to convert analog signals to digital signals for transmission and reconvert signals upon reception at the remote site while allowing for the signal to be compressed for less expensive transmission.

Compressed Video: When video signals are downsized to allow travel along a smaller carrier.

Compression: Reducing the amount of visual information sent in a signal by only transmitting changes in action.

Computer Assisted Instruction (CAI): Teaching process in which a computer is utilized to enhance the learning environment by assisting students in gaining mastery over a specific skill.

Courseware: Often called a learning management system, this is instructional software delivered on a computer that allows for organization and delivery of course material.

Cyberspace: The nebulous "place" where humans interact over computer networks. Coined by William Gibson in Neuromancer.

Desktop Videoconferencing: Videoconferencing on a personal computer.

Digital: An electrical signal that varies in discrete steps in voltage, frequency, amplitude, locations, etc .... Digital signals can be transmitted faster and more accurately than analog signals.

Digital Video Interface (DVI): A video display interface that is used to connect a video source to a video display (such as a monitor or projector).

Distance Education: The process of providing instruction when students and instructors are separated by physical distance and technology.

Distance Learning: The desired outcome of distance education.

Download: Using the network to transfer files from one computer to another.

Echo Cancellation: The process of eliminating the acoustic echo in a video conferencing room.

Electronic Mail (E-mail): Sending messages from one computer user to another.

Facsimile (FAX): System used to transmit textual or graphical images over standard telephone lines.

Fiber Optic Cable: Glass fiber that is used for laser transmission of video, audio, and/or data.

File Transfer Protocol (FTP): A protocol that allows you to move files from a distant computer to a local computer using a network.

Flaming: T.

Frequency: The space between waves in a signal. The amount of time between waves passing a stationary point.

Frequently Asked Questions (FAQ) : A collection of information on the basics of any given subject.

Full Motion Video: Signal which allows transmission of complete action taking place at the origination site.

Fully Interactive Video: (Two way interactive video) Two sites interact with audio and video as if they were co-located.

High Definition Multimedia Interface (HDMI): an audio/video interface for transmitting video with audio to a display.

Home Page: A document with an address (URL) on the World Wide Web maintained by a person or organization which contains pointers to other pieces of information.

Host: A network computer that can receive information from other computers.

Hypertext Markup Language (HTML): The code used to create a home page and is used to access documents over the WWW.

Hypertext Transfer Protocol (HTTP): The protocol used to signify an Internet site is a WWW site, i.e. HTTP is a WWW address.

Hypertext (also called Hyperlink): A document which has been coded to allow a user to select words or pictures within the document, click on them, and connect to further information.

Instructional Design: Creating or selecting learning experiences for a course.

Integrated Services Digital Network (ISDN): A telecommunications standard allowing communications channels to carry voice, video, and data simultaneously.

Interactive Media: Frequency assignment that allows for a two-way interaction or exchange of information.

Learning Management System (LMS): Course management software used to deliver an online course.

Listserv: An e-mail program that allows multiple computer users to connect onto a single system, creating an online discussion.

Live Streaming: Also called simply Streaming, refers to transmitting and/or receiving video content over the Internet. Live Streaming is typically transmitted and received in real time, whereas streaming is typically asynchronous.

Local Area Network (LAN): Two or more local computers that are connected.

Multimedia: Any document which uses multiple forms of communication, such as text, audio, and/or video.

Multi-Point Control Unit (MCU): Computerized switching system which allows point-to-multipoint videoconferencing.

Netiquette: A.

Network: A series of points connected by communication channels in different locations.

Online: Active and prepared for operation. Also suggests access to a computer network.

Origination Site: The location from which a teleconference originates.

Point of Presence (POP): Point of connection between an interexchange carrier and a local carrier to pass communications into the network.

Point-to-Point: Transmission between two locations.

Point-to-Multipoint: Transmission among multiple locations using a bridge.

Protocol : A formal set of standards, rules, or formats for exchanging data that assures uniformity between computers and applications.

Satellite TV: Video and audio signals that are relayed via a communication device that orbits around the earth.

Server: A computer with a special service function on a network, generally receiving and connecting incoming information traffic.

Synchronous: Communication in which interaction among participants is simultaneous.

Telecommunication: The science of information transport using wire, radio, optical, or electromagnetic channels to transmit and receive signals for voice or data communications using electrical means. Teleconferencing: Two way electronic communication among two or more groups in separate locations via audio, video, and/or computer systems.

Transmission Control Protocol (TCP): A protocol which makes sure that packets of data are shipped and received in the intended order.

Transponder: Satellite transmitter and receiver that receives and amplifies a signal prior to re-transmission to an earth station.

Uniform Resource Locator (URL): The address of a homepage on the WWW.

Upload: The act of moving a saved file into a shared online server/cloud, such as an assignment submission box within an online course.

Uplink: The communication link from the transmitting earth station to the satellite.

Video Graphics Array (VGA): A graphics standard for video display, often used to describe the connector between a video source and video display.

Video Teleconferencing: A teleconference including two way video.

Virtual Reality (VR): An interactive experience that takes place within a simulated environment.

Web Conferencing: A web-based teleconference using an Internet interface.

Webinar: An online training course using web conferencing to deliver content and interact with users.

Wiki: A website that allows for collaborative setup and editing by its users.

World Wide Web (WWW): A graphical hypertext-based Internet tool that provides access to homepages created by individuals, businesses, and other organizations.

Figure 1 Faculty Checklist

Once you've been hired to teach an online course in your field, and have the syllabus and course materials, there is more you need to know. Listed below are some questions to ask the Department Chair or Program Director before you begin compiling materials for your online course.

1. What kind of faculty training is offered? Is this training required? Is an electronic competency test required for faculty and/or for students?

2. Which course management software is used?

3. What kinds of automation are available for the instructor?

4. What are the software and hardware requirements for faculty? What are the software (such as Microsoft Word or Access) and hardware requirements for students?

5. What passwords are needed for course and electronic library access?

6. How much of the course content is proscribed?

7. What are my job responsibilities (online training, course design or updating, office hours, live chat, online departmental meetings, minimum number of days online each week)?

8. How quickly am I expected to respond to student e-mails and postings?

9. What are the limits on class size?

10. Are faculty and students required to post online a certain number of days per week?

11. Is student attendance monitored electronically?

12. How do I get copies of the course texts (request from contact person, bookstore, publisher)?

13. Is exam proctoring required?

14. How are grades submitted (online database, e-mail, fax, paper mail)?

15. Who is my contact person? How does this person prefer to be contacted (phone, e-mail, online trouble-shooting form)?

16. Who are some of the other part-time (and full-time) instructors teaching this course online? Are they willing to assist new adjuncts?

17. Who owns my course?

1.2 Technological Preparation

Once you've gotten the answers to the questions on your check-list, it's time to evaluate your hardware and software. When it comes to computers, count on Murphy's Law: if something can go wrong, it will. So to avoid crises ranging from delayed access to destroyed data; plan ahead. There are also some key pieces of hardware and software that you will need to make your experience in the online classroom run as smoothly as possible. Having confidence in your tools will increase your own confidence. Here are a few tips. Share them with your students, as well:

Virus protection: Virus protection software is a necessity, especially if you plan to download any attachments from students onto your home computer. Virus protection is available online for an annual subscription fee (which may be tax deductible); the two leading providers are McAfee (http://www.mcafee.com/us/) and Norton (http://www.symantec.com). New quality options are being created all of the time, so confer with a computer professional, the distance learning department at your college, or the technology help desk for the latest and best recommendations.

Adware and spyware detection software: Most current computer problems are caused by adware (free software) and spyware (software surreptitiously installed on your computer to track your virtual activity). Among the free tools available to help rid your computer of these electronic parasites are Ad-Aware (https://www.adaware.com/)

and Spybot (https://www.safer-networking.org/products/spybot-free-edition/), which scan your computer and identify intrusive software that is present. Once again, there are many options, so confer with knowledgeable professionals for recommendations.

Surge protection: Be sure you have a good surge protector that will protect your computer during power surges and lightning strikes. Surge protectors have come a long way in recent years, and you can now find very affordable surge protection in a multi-outlet power strip or outlet extender. If you are in an area prone to lightning strikes, you may want to opt for a combination surge protector and battery backup, but for most people a surge protecting power strip is fine. For adequate protection, look for a surge protector that can handle at least 400 joules. For better protection, look for at least 600 joules.

Computer back-ups: Be sure to back up all critical information onto storage devices such as a USB flash drive or external hard drive. USB "flash" drives are also great for portably storing student papers if you work at different computers. No matter where you store student data, though, you must consider privacy of that data as a primary concern. Student data, such as grades and enrollment, is protected, so consider password protecting any external storage device as well as your computer. If you don't have a second computer to use when problems arise, scout out computers you can use if yours fails: at your workplace, at a friend's or relative's house, at the local college or public library, or at a local Internet cafe. Be careful when using a public computer, though, because privacy is paramount.

Internet back-ups: Be sure to always have access to the Internet. Just as you will expect your students to submit their work despite interruptions, your students expect you to submit their grades and feedback even when your home Internet connection goes out. There are several ways around such an outage. First, identify at least two locations you can visit quickly to access the Internet, whether this involves taking a laptop to a local restaurant or coffee shop or using a computer at the public or college library. This will be the most common solution for Internet outages for you. However, if you have access to a strong cellular network where you live, you may want to consider a hot spot device that will allow you to access the Internet through your cellular data service in case of any issues. Service to a hot spot device can often be turned on and off through your cellular provider very quickly, so consult with your service provider to see what options are available. Finally, in a pinch, you can access the Internet through your smartphone or cellular service enabled tablet. These devices do not offer the most comprehensive access, so they are not considered the best option for regular use. However, with so many more resources becoming mobile friendly the utility of mobile devices for teaching online is improving.

Settings: Some of the technological preparations for your online teaching experience will involve changing some settings on your Internet browser. The first of these that you want to check is the status of your popup blocker. Many publisher-provided resources, for example, are on sites outside of your learning management software, and they may require launch in a separate tab or window within your browser. Disabling the popup blocker, at least for the sites you regularly access for your course, will help you to get to the resources you need. You will also want to check the status of your Flash and Java plugins, and make sure they stay up-to-date. This helps not only your access to websites and resources, but the security of your work while visiting or viewing them. Additionally, make sure you keep your computer up to date by either enabling automatic updates or checking for updates regularly.

Adobe Acrobat Reader: PDF files are non-editable, which makes them excellent and frequently used choices for things like articles and online textbooks. You will need to download and keep your Adobe Acrobat Reader or similar PDF reader software up to date.

Microsoft Word or compatible software: Most students will submit written files in Microsoft Word format. Therefore, you need a way to read these files in order to grade them. If you do not have access to Microsoft Office, or specifically Microsoft Word, you can download free compatible reader software or use a free word processor like Google Docs to convert the file into something you can view. Unless you use an Apple computer, you may also have trouble reading Pages files from the built-in word processor on Apple computers. Pages can convert a file to Microsoft Word format, so you may want to request that your students take that step before submitting their work or consider having a program that can convert the file for you.

1.3   Design and Content Preparation

Inexperienced online teachers are often surprised by the amount of time involved not only in creating a course, but also in facilitating it. A 1999-2000 study conducted by Belinda Davis-Lazarus, a faculty member in education at the University of Michigan-Dearborn, gives some insight into the time commitment required. Lazarus's longitudinal case study found that an experienced instructor of three online education courses spent 3.5 to 7.0 hours per week on each course. The time was spent responding to student e-mails, participating in discussions, and grading. The time commitment is generally higher the first time you teach a course than in subsequent semesters, just as it is when you teach face-to-face.

Despite the general belief by college instructors that teaching online takes more time, the data actually suggest that face-to-face courses require slightly more (Van de Vord and Pogue, 2012). Though the hours spent per student per week may be relatively equal between online and face-to-face courses the time is spent quite differently. For example, instead of spending three hours per week lecturing you will spend that time on the computer. You will also be more likely to interact with your students through e-mail or other Internet-based communication than in person. In an online course, you do not have the benefit of seeing your students to gauge their understanding of the material, so much of your time online will be spent grading work to monitor progress and comprehension. Therefore, you will spend more time grading when teaching an online course than you do in a face-to-face course, but the overall time commitment is consistent.

A significant difference in teaching online is that there is much more advanced preparation necessary. Instructors accustomed to deciding what to do in each class session the night before they meet with their students may find the transition overwhelming. An effective and well-organized online classroom is one where all material is posted from the day the course opens. It is possible to build and open a course week by week or module by module, but the best courses are set up and ready to open completely on the first day of the semester. There is quite a bit of discussion among distance learning instructors regarding the pros and cons of actually opening everything from the beginning of the course versus having everything ready but opening the course gradually throughout the semester. Each course and each instructor are different, and you should consider which option works best for the course you will be teaching as you plan. No matter what, though, it is important to have the class designed, planned, and completely ready to start on the first day it is available to students. This may seem daunting at first, but it will save you a great deal of time later on. Here are some tips to help ease the transition to the online classroom:

1. Visit sample online classrooms to get a sense of what works and what doesn't, and to better recognize your own online teaching style. Many colleges offer sample course sites for prospective students to explore and/or for prospective teachers to use as inspiration. Here are a few for the most popular learning management systems, classified according to the course management software used:

A. Canvas
    I. University of Texas Training Center https://utexas.instructure.com/courses/633028/pages/example-canvas-courses?module_item_id=7256980
    II. Pasadena City College 16-Week Course Template https://canvas.pasadena.edu/courses/982220
B. BlackBoard
    I. CUNY Academic Commons https://wiki.commons.gc.cuny.edu/sample_blackboard_courses_and_modules/
    II. BlackBoard Instructor Help https://help.blackboard.com/Learn/Instructor
C. Moodle
    I. Moodle Demo https://moodle.org/demo/
D. D2L (Desire 2 Learn; Brightspace)
    I. Accessible Templates https://distancelearning.elgin.edu/d2l-tutorials/d2l_10_3_faculty_guides/en/accessible-html-templates.html

2. Start simply. You don't have to incorporate all the technological bells and whistles as you begin; trying to do so will only overwhelm you. For example, if you want to incorporate live chat, but aren't sure about how it will work, you can make such interaction an option in your first course rather than a requirement. Once you understand the technology, you'll feel better able to construct a more intricate system of group activities and discussions.

3. Set consistent deadlines. Make deadlines absolute, and consistently apply your policy. Remember, attendance in an online course is usually measured by work submitted by students, not how often they log into the course. Therefore, students must stay on top of the required work to be successful. To allow for the challenges that life frequently presents,

consider dropping the lowest grade within groups of assignments (such as tests, discussions, or projects) or allowing students to submit late work for reduced credit. When employing discussion boards or other multi-step assignments, you may want to consider more frequent deadlines. For example, the students may be required to submit their initial discussion board post before the end of the day on Tuesday but have until Friday to reply to their classmates for credit, or they may submit a rough draft of a writing assignment for peer review on Wednesday and the final version on Sunday.

4. Set a schedule and stick to it. Distance learning instructors often face the same types of time management issues that students face. It is very easy to procrastinate on grading or checking discussion boards when you do not have set class times to follow. Therefore, it is important to set a schedule. For the instructor, though, there are two parts to the schedule. The first part is the schedule set for students, which should be clear and easily understood information about what is being covered, what assignments are due, and when the work must be submitted. Consider the timing of your deadlines carefully when making this schedule. For example, if you are not someone who is normally awake at midnight, do not set a deadline for midnight. You will inevitably face a situation in which a student has trouble with an assignment submission attempted too close to the deadline, and handling that in the middle of the night may not be in your best interest. The second part of the schedule is your own work schedule. Set consistent hours that you will dedicate to grading, office hours (whether in person or online), and other course tasks. Set deadlines for grading the different types of assignments you include in your course, communicate the deadlines to your students, and commit to sticking to them. If you intend to have papers graded within one week of the deadline, then make sure you schedule the time to complete the work within that time frame. Consistency and communication build trust with students, making them more likely to rely on you for other things when they need help.

5. Seek training. There are many free training resources available, and it is likely that your college distance learning department has some available as well. Online webinars are frequently available through textbook publisher websites and many professional organizations offer trainings both in person and online. If there is type of resource or technology that is new to you, seek out videos on YouTube or the website for the resource that can show you how it works. Consult with

colleagues who may be willing to help, and take full advantage of any training or support offered to online instructors at your institution.

1.4 Tips for Working Efficiently

To save time, set limits on the time spent on the computer; encourage more student-to-student interaction, and make better use of time-saving technology and strategies. Here are some specific suggestions:

◄ Block out times during which you will be available to students. Communicate these times to your students.

◄ Have students post their pictures in an introductory post or add an avatar through their Learning Management System profile. Updating the Learning Management profile is an easy addition to an orientation assignment. Students are often familiar with this process from creating social media profiles.

◄ Don't respond to every student on a discussion board. Allow students to moderate discussions; they can answer each other's publicly posted questions. In fact, if you respond too quickly, you can inhibit student responses.

◄ Have students collaborate on group projects. This results in interactions that don't involve the instructor, and in fewer papers to grade. It also helps to build a course community.

◄ Consider the format of the assignments you include. Is a lengthy writing assignment, essay or discussion board post truly the best way to assess understanding for every topic, or could you consider having students fill in a template or table instead?

Put Out the Flames

◄ Make sure that the ideas of online etiquette, or "netiquette," are clear.

◄ Remind students to be patient and to forgive others' missteps.

◄ Set parameters for appropriate behaviors.

◄ Discuss the challenges associated with online communication.

◀ Use computer-graded quizzes and assignments whenever possible. Consider self-grading quiz tools for more than just quizzes. Learning management systems all have a quiz tool available that is set as self-grading. You can also use this tool for other assignments that you want to be self-grading. For example, you might create a "checklist quiz" that requires students to acknowledge that they have completed each assignment due within a week or module. You might also consider a Reading Quiz to check with the student regarding any reading assignments for the module.

◀ Consider breaking large projects into smaller pieces. For example, if you have a ten-page paper included in your course, have students submit pieces of it throughout the semester. This will help them stay on track and improve the quality of their work, which ultimately reduces your grading time once the final submission is in your hands.

◀ Consider using a peer review format on some assignments so the students are giving each other feedback before you grade it. They will often identify the same issues you will, and they learn from the process of editing.

◀ Save and reuse your discussion board postings from one semester to the next.

◀ Avoid busy work. Make sure every assignment in your course is meaningful and consistent with your course goals.

◀ If you require citations in a particular format (MLA, APA, etc.) include a tutorial and/or set of examples. List textbook information in your required citation format in your syllabus. Tell students to use it as a guide. Provide links to reliable online citation generators if one of your goals is that students learn proper citation. Citation generators are easy to find with a quick Internet search.

◀ Create a file of announcements, messages, and snippets of text to reuse. Label your announcements and messages clearly (e.g. "Week 1 Assignments" or "E-mail to students who missed assignment one"). Maintain at least one document of bits of text that you frequently use in assignment feedback or discussion comments. Recycle this content quickly and easily as needed.

◄ Create and maintain a FAQ (Frequently Asked Questions). Update this page often to keep it relevant. Refer students to this page often and make it easy to find within your online course.

◄ When teaching multiple sections of the same course, use the same syllabus, assignments, or other resources. Consider creating these materials in an easily shared and updated format such as Google Drive. If you do this, and you need to make an update or correction, you only make it once and all of your sections have instant access. Google Sheets (similar to Microsoft Excel) is a good option for maintaining course calendars in a similar way and has many calendar and checklist templates that can make this a very easy transition.

◄ Set clear expectations for the course and each assignment at the start of the course, and frequently repeat common instructions. It is often helpful to include a reminder to review syllabi and course schedules when sending weekly announcements. This will help you to save time by avoiding clarifications later on.

◄ Assemble a body of Internet links related to your course, and build on it each semester through your own searches, as well as by assigning students to compile and annotate a list of course-related Web sites. These can be collected from students as an assignment, with the added benefit of eventually building a comprehensive set of resources. These can be collected in a wiki (discussed in Chapter 3), a shared document (Google Drive is a great free re-source for this), or an online bulletin board such as Padlet (www. padlet.com) or Pinterest (www.pinterest.com).

◄ Have assignments due at mid-week rather than at the end of the week, especially if you want to stay away from the computer during the weekend.

◄ Find it before you make it. Before creating resources from scratch, scour the Internet for things that other instructors may have shared, check with your textbook publisher to see what they have available, and consult with colleagues who may let you use their resources. Also, consult with an instructional librarian at your college to help you locate resources. For example, organizations such as Khan Academy (https://www. khanacademy.org/) and TED (https://ed.ted.com/) have well-made and accurately captioned videos on a variety of topics that are available to use in your courses. Check the copyright permissions carefully before using resources that you find to make sure you are allowed to use them for academic purposes. There are many resources out there that are open resources, free to use by anyone.

◄ Pre-schedule messages such as reminders to send automatically whenever possible. Many learning management systems have this function, and there are free online resources if yours does not. One great resource is Remind (www.remind.com) that allows you to schedule messages ahead to send out as text messages or e-mails to students on the date and at the time you desire.

◄ Create and use rubrics or grading guides for assignments. Not only does this let a student know how to be successful, but it helps to save time in grading complex assignments.

◄ Make sure students have passed an orientation quiz or completed an online scavenger hunt at the start of the semester so that they know how to navigate the course; this will reduce the number of questions later. If your school offers an orientation to online courses for students, direct your students to complete it before beginning work in your course.

◄ Require that students send work as .txt (text) files if formatting is not an issue, and as .rtf (rich text format) files when formatting is important. This will minimize your download time, and problems related to software conflicts.

◄ Bookmark the site you use to access your course and write down the password information and tech help phone number; keep both near your computer and in your wallet for when you're working remotely on a computer where this information has not been saved. Save it on your phone as well. Bookmark the sites you use to access any resources used outside of your course, such as publisher-provided resources or reminder services.

Chapter Two

Teaching the Online Student

2.1   Profile of the Online Learner

The number of students who enroll in online courses has increased significantly in recent years. Historically, the learners in online courses tended to be older working adults with a demanding and competing set of responsibilities, including full-time jobs, families and school (National Center for Education Statistics, 2018). However, college student populations are becoming more diverse. Your online classroom is likely to have students of a variety of ages, ranging from high school students to older adults returning to college after spending time in the workforce. In addition to a wide range of ages, the number of first generation college students has increased dramatically. Researchers estimate that as many as 30 percent of today's college students are first generation (Opidee, 2015). These first generation students are more likely to enroll in online courses (Postsecondary National Policy Institute, 2018).

Successful online college students need to have at least some computer skills. Many colleges do not require students to demonstrate technological proficiency before enrolling in an online course, resulting in underprepared students attempting an online course without the skills necessary to compete them successfully. Many colleges, however, do provide support or screening tools that the students can access, even if they are not required. For example, Pitt Community College in Greenville, North Carolina, has an online resource that gives students a chance to self-evaluate their computer skills and walks the students through using the college's LMS. This is done through an online course that is both free for all students to complete and in which students are automatically and continuously enrolled. Students can, therefore, access the preparation course and the resources included within it at any time. Online student support is commonly available to students at many colleges, but remember that this type of support is often not required and depends on students being self-motivated to access it.

"Self-regulated learners are aware when they know a fact or possess a skill and when they do not. Self-regulated students proactively seek out information when needed and take steps to master it" (Zimmerman, 1990). Self-regulation is a key skill for successful online students. Referring back to the diversity of today's classroom, it is important to consider that you may have many students who are not self-directed. For example, adult students may not have all of the required computer skills needed to be successful; continuing students may be proficient in using some forms of technology but might not be proficient at using the technology needed to be a strong student. First generation American students may not be ready to be self-directed learners. This makes it critical that you develop an online course that is easy to navigate and one that encourages all students to develop the skills necessary to become self-regulated learners.

As students increase their ability to be self-regulated, your efforts to teach them will become more effective, allowing you to create an environment where you can guide and facilitate the learning. Remember to include learning activities that involve students actively in the learning process. For example, students may prefer the self- discovery of a project to watching a video of you lecturing. Students respond well to diagnosing their own strengths and weaknesses and being guided toward greater mastery in their weaker areas; they appreciate a more individualized program of self-improvement, whenever possible.

2.2 Handling Student Conflicts

While self-directed learners tend to be eager students, they can also have high expectations for the course and the instructor. When these expectations are added on top of the pressures of competing responsibilities that our students are facing, conflicts can arise. Online, such conflict may take the form of nasty e-mails and angry postings. Clashes can erupt as a result of low grades, confusion related to assignments, and the student's own poor organizational skills.

It is important to prevent as many of these types of conflicts as possible by preparing a strong syllabus, course and chapter objectives, clear assignments, and grading rubrics. Each of these topics are covered in later chapters.

One thing that you can do to help facilitate the development of self-regulated learners in your classroom is to invite them to make suggestions for course policies in an online discussion forum. Students will often agree to reasonable rules of behavior when they are allowed to set the parameters themselves. As the instructor, you may need to guide their conversations and should make sure that they know that you have the final approval for the final course policies.

It is important to allow for discussions with students about behavior that is appropriate in an online classroom community. You might ask students to research and share the best tips that they find for working in an online environment. This type of thing can be easily incorporated into an orientation assignment or discussion forum within your course. Giving students a chance to contribute their ideas creates a sense of ownership of the online course community.

It is likely that, at some point, a student will approach you inappropriately. It is important to be sure to respond calmly and politely, and it may be necessary to take a step back from the situation before responding. For example, if you receive a nasty note about the unfairness of a grade, write back and say that you're always willing to discuss issues if approached in a friendly and professional manner, and that you'd be glad to chat if the student would like to send a more appropriate message. This defuses a potentially explosive situation and an apology usually follows. The student has cooled off by that point and is more likely to recognize how the note came across.

If a student "flames," or attacks, another student, step in quickly by either removing the post (if needed) or with a public posting that reminds students about netiquette. Reply privately to the attacker that the postings were inappropriate and to the victim that you are handling the situation.

It is important, as the instructor in an online course, to be as proactive as possible regarding course conflict. Creating thorough and easy to find resources and guidelines for students to follow will reduce the amount of conflict that you encounter. Easily accessed student conduct policies will also provide students with advance notice of consequences of their actions.

The best way to avoid conflict, though, is to be "present" in the online classroom. Resist the urge to create a course than can essentially run itself...a "set it and forget it" course. Let the students know you are there and monitoring their participation and actions. Also, deal with issues that arise with students privately as often as possible before you post public messages. Be sensitive to the students, and understand that their actions, though inappropriate and unacceptable within your course, are likely the results of stressors that are not visible to you within the course environment. Follow your own policies so the students can trust that you will follow the rules, but reach out to students who are clearly struggling as well.

2.3 Plagiarism and Test Security

As the popularity of online courses grows, so does the opportunity for cheating. It seems as though as soon as one type of security measure is put into place, students discover a way to work around it. Let's start by looking at some of the statistics about cheating from the Open Educational Database:

- 60.8 percent of college students admit to cheating
- 85 percent of students think cheating is essential
- 95 percent of students do not get caught
- Cheaters have higher GPAs
- Cheating is likely to have started in high school

These numbers paint a troubling picture. The online environment makes it easier than ever for students to copy information from other sources and present it as their own. This often leads to a violation of copyright and plagiarism. Students are also masters of searching for test answers while completing online quizzes and tests, and there are many websites out there to help them do it. Additionally, there is an entire industry dedicated to purchasing papers and writing assignments written by someone else, and many students do not feel that this is a form of cheating.

It is important to plan your course under the assumption that you have the highest respect and regard for your students. Convey this message to them clearly and often. You may want to reiterate a policy against copying information from outside sources in each of your assignments. Have a clear policy in your syllabus to deal with this issue, including examples and consequences of each type of academic dishonesty that you include. At the same time, create safeguards to prevent cheating as often as possible.

Some common strategies for avoiding academic dishonesty include:

- **Randomized tests**: Use courseware that allows you to randomize the order of test and quiz questions and answers, and to pull questions from a test bank that includes more questions than you require on the test so that each student's test is different.

- **Limited test functions**: To discourage sharing of tests, use any available courseware functions that prohibit printing of test pages, that reveal only one test question at a time, and that do not reveal the test questions on the graded exam (either at all or at least until the deadline for the exam has passed).

- **Timed tests**: Timed tests also discourage sharing. By limiting the time available to take the test, you limit the amount of time students have to search for the answers and ensure that they must know at least a minimum of information to complete the test. A good guideline for a multiple-choice test is to set a limit that allows for no more than one minute per question.

- **Personal input**: Ask questions that require students to illustrate a concept with examples from their own experiences instead of simply providing a "correct" answer.

- **New tests**: Rewrite all of your test questions each semester or keep multiple test banks that you can alternate for each new course.

- **Group tests**: Allow collaboration on an untimed test.

- **Oral tests**: Give "chat" tests in which you question each student online about course concepts.

- **Ungraded self-tests**: Increase students' confidence levels— and suppress the feeling that they must cheat to pass—by providing plenty of opportunities for self-testing to let them know if they have mastered the course concepts; for these kinds of tests, use multiple choice, true -false, or matching so that students can easily grade themselves.

- **Varied test types**: Give different sorts of tests, including both timed and untimed, proctored and unproctored, individual and group, as well as formats such as multiple choice, true/false, fill-in-the blank, short-answer, and essay.

- **Unusual paper topics**: For research papers, provide a list of unusual assignment topics from which students can choose. Encourage original, critical thinking by asking students to try to answer unresolved questions such as "What is the best way to solve our current energy crisis?" or "Why is the U.S. so politically divided?" or "Which South American country would be most suitable to host the Summer Olympics?"

- **Provide a specific case study for analysis**: Instead of simply gathering information, students will have to use what they learn to provide their own insights.

- **Recipe assignments**: Require an annotated bibliography or a particular documentation style. You can also create a "recipe" for each assignment. One paper, for example, might require a table, photograph, or illustration; a personally conducted survey or interview; and eight sources, all within the last fifteen years and three within the last five years. In addition, all sources must be attached to the assignment.

- **Assignments in stages**: For students with poor time-management skills who feel pressured to cheat because they run out of time, structure assignments in stages. It's also helpful to set a due date early in the semester, before students are overwhelmed with assignments for other courses.

- **Post-assignment discussion**: Once a paper is turned in, ask students specific questions about their topics and papers, and how they conducted their research. You can also ask students to write short essays about what they learned from completing an assignment. If you prefer a less formal approach, require an online group discussion about an assignment, or request an individual response about the assignment from each student via phone or e-mail. Require multiple short assignments in lieu of one longer paper or test.

- **Research instructions**: Clarify to students how to use information gathered online. Help them to use the technology without copying it by setting up their own databases, which might include the source, subject, keywords, and abstract. You can also help students by leading them to your library's online databases, which are often password-protected and thus a bit harder to reach until students request the passwords from the library. Without such guidance, students will be more likely to conduct general Web searches, and to stumble upon complete essays they may find too tempting to resist.

- **Familiarity with student writing**: Through discussion board postings and other informal assignments (which would not be likely to be plagiarized), you can come to know your students' writing and thinking abilities. As a result, it becomes much easier to recognize work that is not the students' own. If you utilize a written "icebreaker," it may be of value in identifying the authenticity of student writing.

It is important to note that students are not the only ones who easily fall prey to plagiarism and copyright violation. It is very easy for you, as an instructor, to use content that you do not have the rights to use. This content may be a video or an assignment that you find online, or it could be an article that you find in a database.

It is always a good idea to search for ideas and resources online, but before you use content off of the Internet, be sure that you are allowed to do so. If you have questions about this, there are many great resources about copyright online or you could contact your college's distance learning department or library. There are growing numbers of open educational resources available for instructors to use, so it is not likely to be difficult to find an option that is free and permissible to use in your course.

Chapter Three

TECHNOLOGY

The increased availability and use of technology in recent years ranks among the most dramatic changes in education. One need merely walk through a university building and view the number of computer labs and students on laptops, smartphones, and tablets to grasp this fact. It may, at times, feel as though there are too many technological options available for incorporation into one's online courses. Without proper planning, it is easy to become overwhelmed with the choices and begin to incorporate technologies that are not actually the best options to meet your lesson and course goals.

It is important to consider the kinds of technological resources your students have available to them. While some colleges provide students with laptops and a standard suite of software, this is not the norm. Students will access your online course using different connections, browsers and devices. **This means that before integrating types of technology in your courses, first determine how accessible the tools will be to your students, whether the tools are the appropriate one for achieving your lesson and course goals, and whether the tools are reliable.**

Another issue to consider related to technology is how proficient both you and your students are with working with the types of resources you make available. One strategy employed by colleges is to make basic technology training available to students. There are tutorials that show students how to upload an assignment, submit to a discussion board, create and upload a video, and more. Distance learning and IT departments provide similar tutorials for instructors, as well as more in-depth training and consultation.

If such a course is not available for your students, consider assigning practice exercises at the start of the course to help students to troubleshoot issues before they reach graded assignments. You may also consider providing a course readiness checklist that allows students to see what kinds of skills and resources they will need to be successful in your course.

To be successful as an online instructor, you must view technology as an asset—not a detriment to good communication with students. It is crucial to provide consistent feedback to all students. Most important, of course, you must be alert very early to identify students who may be having trouble, not due to their capability, but due to their difficulty with the technology. Provide the students with enough tools to communicate with you efficiently and effectively, but avoid the trap of providing technology simply to have it included. Sometimes a new technology is not the best option, and including it just because it is the "latest thing" is never a good reason to include it. **Match your technology with the needs and goals of the course. Use the training and resources available to you and keep a close watch on students who may be struggling.**

Below is a list of the tools of distance education that you'll need to be able to use and to which you'll need to have access:

3.1 Internet

A fast, reliable online connection is vital to your work as an online instructor. Connecting via DSL (digital subscriber line) or cable is the standard. However, connecting via wifi is more often what your students will do, and what you may do as well. More available Internet connections, including smartphone Internet access, mean that when a student contacts you with a question, you can easily and quickly log on to the course for reference.

You need unlimited Internet access, which has become the industry standard. Be sure that your ISP (Internet Service Provider) is reliable and offers around-the-clock technical support. Also, identify at least two places you can go for access if your home access is disrupted, and consider having your students do the same.

In addition to basic Internet access on your laptop or desktop computer, accessing the Internet through a smartphone and/or tablet is an increasingly important tool. Be aware, though, that many sites are not optimized for mobile browser viewing and many learning management systems are not set up to allow you to complete quizzes or assignments through smartphones or tablets. Distance learning professionals on your campus can give you the best information about mobile compatibility. Forward this information to your students. Many students use tablets to take their online courses, and you do not want to run into an issue that prevents a student from completing an assignment because they do not have a compatible Internet connection.

3.2   E-mail

If your course software includes e-mail, direct your students to use it to contact you; this helps keep all the communication for each course in one spot, and makes for easy referencing later. If the college for which you're teaching gives you a college e-mail address, use that account for all communication with college personnel and students, and be sure that you know how to access the account remotely. If you do have a college e-mail account, remember to check it daily. In most cases, a student's college e-mail account is considered a valid and official method of communication, meaning that there are enough identity checks in place to satisfy privacy laws and guidelines. Do not discuss grades with a student through their personal e-mail or other outside communication unless you can be absolutely certain that you are communicating privately with the student. Student privacy must always be taken into account when communicating, and you will find that e-mail is the most common way a student will reach out to you.

One other reminder about e-mail—sort mail into folders (one for each class or for each student) for easy management. Dr. Gary Wheeler, writing in *A Handbook for Adjunct/Part-Time Faculty and Teachers of Adults* (Greive, 2011), gives some excellent advice for using e-mail with students. It is: "Establish processes and expectations for e-mail use by your students that include guidelines regarding tone of language, frequency, educational purpose, and format."

3.3   Instant Messaging

Instant messaging, or IM, refers to text messages or other messages sent in real time, a method by which you and a student can instantly contact each other when you are both online. There are many instant messaging services from which to choose, and many are built into systems already available to you. For example, if your institution uses a Gmail based e-mail system, students automatically have access to Google Hangouts with their student accounts. A separate Facebook, WhatsApp, or Twitter account used only for your courses can give you other options. You can also consider a service such as Remind (www.remind.com) that communicates by text message without revealing any phone numbers. Skype is another popular option, and it also allows for video conferencing both individually and in groups. Don't forget to look at what is built into your learning management system as well. For example, Blackboard has a program called Collaborate that allows for communication with students as well as chat room style functioning. Moodle also has a messaging function.

If you've told students which program you're using, how to find you there, and when you'll be online, they can send you questions during that time; an instant message will pop up on your computer or smartphone, and you can answer immediately. You might want to set up your computer to notify you by sound whenever you have a message, and consider setting up your smartphone with a unique ringtone for the app students use to contact you in this way. By setting up a unique ringtone, you will be sure to know when the notification is from a student so you can respond accordingly.

3.4 Chat Rooms

Chat rooms and web conferences are good places for student teams to discuss projects in real time; assign group roles when a group first forms. Deal with conflicts as they arise. Encourage students to interact through a space on your site or in temporary chat rooms (such as through Google Hangouts, Zoom, or Yahoo). Make sure that students always provide you with a transcript or recording of their chat or conference sessions so that you can monitor their progress.

You can also use the chat room for online office hours. Enter a designated chat room and keep that window open on your desktop so that you can answer questions from any student who enters at that time. You can also schedule study sessions or exam review sessions through chat rooms, and in some cases you can deliver course material through live lectures using chat rooms (which can often be recorded and posted for those students who could not attend the live feed).

One thing to consider when employing chat rooms is whether your class is considered synchronous or asynchronous. An asynchronous class is the norm for distance learning, and means that there are no scheduled meetings of any kind. Adding a synchronous (scheduled) component to an asynchronous course can be difficult, so try to avoid scheduled online meetings or lectures unless your course specifically outlines them in the registration course schedule. This does not mean that you cannot use chat rooms or web conferencing. It simply means you cannot make a scheduled meeting a requirement. Instead, create lectures through web conferencing. Record the lectures and upload them. You can hold office hours through chat rooms; encourage students to use them for study teams and schedule optional review sessions.

3.5 Blogs

Short for "web logs," blogs are public journals available online through blog sites or on personal Web sites. They are also increasingly available through learning management system software. Their appeal is that they are easily updated and provide a way to follow personal stories, as well as to measure social temperatures on current issues. You can use them in your teaching as writing or reading assignments, and you may want to read and even participate in blogs related to teaching online. A free, easy tool to have your students create and post their own blogs is available at http://www.blogger.com . Other popular free blog sites are www.wordpress.com and www.wix.com. Because a blog posted outside of your course software is a public record available to anyone with Internet access, blog postings are different from discussion board postings. The larger audience and the more personal nature of blogs make them an option to offer students interested in creating something that will last beyond the end of the term.

3.6 Listservs

Automated mailing lists, listservs allow for discussions via e-mail on specialized topics of interest. You can seek advice about problems you are having in the online classroom by joining a distance education listserv. While inactive listservs aren't very helpful, those that dump hundreds of messages a day into your inbox quickly become impossible to manage, so you may want to try out a few services before you settle on the one that best matches your needs. See the section on "Listservs and other discussion forums" near the end of this handbook for some specific listserv resource suggestions.

3.7 Wikis

A wiki is a website on which participants collaboratively include and update content. Wiki's are rapidly replacing listservs as collaborative tools between professionals, and they can be useful resources for teaching as well. Joining a wiki through an organization that focuses on distance learning for educators can help you to access up-to-date information without the e-mail bombardment that comes with many listservs. Wikipedia is probably the most famous wiki, and the bane of many instructors' grading experiences. It has given us a valuable place to start when researching, but too often is the only place students look for information. This is a problem because accuracy checks have historically been limited to other contributors. However, the accuracy of information Wikipedia is improving, and the same is true for other wiki resources.

You can use a wiki in your class by creating a site for students to edit together. For example, you may assign a team project that requires students to create a website that educates the public on some important issue. With a wiki, the students can work together to create the resource, check each other for accuracy, and experience a meaningful learning activity. You can also access the wikis easily to check progress. Wikis are often available within learning management systems, so there may not be a need to create on on an outside website. Check your own course software to see if a wiki is available as an assignment.

As an instructor, you can use a wiki to create a course calendar that you can easily keep updated, provide resources for each topic that you can update frequently, or collaborate with peers teaching the same course to create a joint set of resources. There are many ways to use wikis, and the best benefit of them is their ease of access and use.

3.8   Discussion Forums

Many websites have discussion forums for members to use to discuss relevant topics. Instructors often use the built-in discussion forum applications within learning management systems as assignments, but they can also be used as areas for questions, general discussions, and student-to-student contact. Most learning management systems offer different types of subscriptions which determine whether students automatically receive e-mails including new posts, have control over whether they receive e-mails or daily/weekly digests of posts, or are only subscribed to receive posts if they have posted to the forum themselves. Setting up a forum with automatic subscriptions for students can be an excellent way to make announcements that are accessible for the entire course in case they are deleted from e-mail accounts prematurely.

Discussion forums outside of your course are excellent places to seek advice, help, and resources in your efforts to design and deliver your online course. Joining communities of online educators provides you with a group of peers, and you may even find a group dedicated to educators of your specific discipline.

"Don't Poke Me: Professors' Privacy In The Age Of Facebook"

by Rich Russell

Unlike my students, I remember a world without social networking. I joined Facebook back before moms did, when it was still the semi-elite space of college students. Now it's a place for everyone. I thought I would offer my brief note on the matter when it comes to the 21st century dilemma of to friend or not to friend one's students. I do not: not current students anyway.

If a student requests to be my "friend" after grades have been entered for the semester (the word friend itself seems odd: are we friends? As Henry James would offer, "We are not enemies."), then I might accept, because my own page is rather tame/boring; mostly I post nothing more than links to articles. And it is natural to feel responsible for one's students long after the term expires. It seems a good way to continue that advisory role we must undertake as educators. But while the students are still in my class or have registered for one of my classes again — why Facebook (verb) them?

And while it has become selfish to want a life of one's own these days, I still do want one. I deny current students access to my Facebook wall. This is what I feel is appropriate....

(Originally published by AdjunctNation.com and used here with permission.)

Chapter Four
COURSE DEVELOPMENT
AND PLANNING

When developing and planning your course, much will depend on what you are given to as a starting point. If your course has already been created, and you have to use it as it is, you may simply need to substitute your personal information in the required areas and you will be good to go. If you're given another instructor's course as a model, you may have more freedom to make changes in both the nature of the course assignments and in course design. If you are asked to start from scratch, this gives you the most freedom in your course design, but may be the most difficult option if you have never taught online before.

You may also have access to a master course from which you can download information and assignments or you may have access to a course pack from the publisher to provide some of the required information and required work. Many times these publisher course packs are customizable and you can include relevant information while leaving out work that does not suit you or your course. Overriding the decisions of what to include in your course will always be dictated by the requirements of the college where you are teaching. Some schools will give you *carte blanche* while other schools will require strict adherence to a provided course outline, or somewhere in between.

If you are given a course template, there might be certain design requirements and a general syllabus, but you may be expected to do a lot of the actual course building. However, there is always a chance that you will be expected to build a course from scratch.

Most courses will be divided by either chapters, modules or units of work, and the organization of the course is the best place to start. Your syllabus is the road map of your course. It sets the expectations and requirements for both you and your students. It is important that your write your syllabus in clear language and that you are consistent throughout your syllabus. Having inconsistencies or loopholes in your syllabus will lead to problems down the road.

Figure 2 Model Distance Ed. Syllabus

Course Information

Course title: The official name of your course as it is listed in your college's catalog.

Course number: The unique identifier for your course which is provided by the college.

Course description: It is essential that you take the course description from your college's catalog. Your course description must match the one provided by your college not only for consistency, but for accreditation purposes too.

Credit hours: This is the number of credits your course is worth. Again, this information is found in your college's catalog.

Location: This course will be completely online, no student meetings are required.

Course dates: This section is optional.

Local Prerequisite(s): You will find this information in the college catalog.

Instructor Information

Name: Put your name here as you wish to be addressed. For example, if you want to be called Dr., Ms. or Mr. use that name here.

E-mail: Always use your official college e-mail address here. This is critical to maintain confidentiality and to have a record of contacts with the students in case there is a problem down the line.

Virtual office hours: This may not be required- check with your school on this policy.

Phone number: You may be hesitant to share your phone number with your students. If this is a case, think about using an app like Remind that allows you to contact your students via text while protecting your phone number.

Required Instructional Material

Required Textbook: Be sure to give the full title and edition of the text you are using. Many students will purchase or rent the textbook from somewhere other than the college bookstore. This information is essential to ensure that they have the correct book.

Course Expectations

This is the area that you will list the goals for the course; you'll outline in detail what students can expect to learn in your class.

Course Objectives

There will be two different sets of objectives for your class. You will have the overarching course objectives, these are driven by the course description you pulled from the college catalog earlier. You may add in other course objectives, but you must include the ones from the course description. You will also have a set of objectives for each module, chapter or unit. These unit objectives must align to your course objectives.

Attendance Policy

As with any other type of class, you will be expected to have an attendance policy. Many colleges require you to verify attendance in a class as part of financial aid. So, this makes it critical that you have a policy.

There are two schools of thought in creating your attendance policy: student logins and students submitting work. Most LMS allow you to see the last login date of your students, so this could be the driver for your policy. Or, if you have at least one assignment due a week, you can use the submission of assignments as verification of attendance. Either way, it is important to make sure that your policy is clear, easy to understand and follow, and that is does not have any grey areas to it. Here is a sample attendance policy for you to review:

Participation is the lifeblood of an online class. You are expected to participate in weekly discussions, to keep up with deadlines for other assignments, and to check your e-mail at least every other day. You must log into this course a minimum of once a week (more often is strongly suggested). Students who do not log in to the course for 7 consecutive days or contact me to talk about their absence will be dropped from this class.

Grading Policy

Is your school on a ten-point scale? Does it allow you to issue plus and minus with the letter grades? This is the area that you explain the grading policy for students. You will also include information on the various assignments in the class and how they will impact a student's overall grade Add a simple pie chart graphic here to help students see how much the various assignments contribute to their final grade. This simple graphic catches the eye and provides important course information quickly.

Late work policy:

It is important to think through your late work policy for your online class very carefully as once you have created one, it is critical to apply is fairly to all students. Here are some common ideas to get you thinking about your late work policy:

- Having soft and hard deadlines (give students bonus points for meeting the earlier, soft deadline).
- Allowing one free pass to turn in late work.
- Dropping the lowest grade on a category of assignments.

It is important to encourage students not to wait until the last minute to complete work. However, we all know that some students tend to wait until it is too late. Other students may experience technical issues. Allowing some leniency in your policy can turn a disaster into a teachable moment for the student.

Instructor Response Times: Online courses tend to be asynchronous, so it is critical for you, as the instructor, to have a clear policy on your response times. It is just as important to make sure that your students understand this information. This does not mean that you need to be online 24/7, it actually is the opposite. By posting a clear response policy (and following it), you are setting appropriate boundaries. As you create this policy, be sure to include response times to all types of activities: e-mails, messages in your LMS, grading and feedback on assignments and any other type of activity your course contains. Create a policy that is realistic for your to meet as it is important that you follow this policy for the semester.

Students with Disabilities Statement: Check with your school and/ or department for their disability statement. You will be posting your syllabus online, so feel free to link to the policy and the webpage for your Office of Disability Services. By linking to this information, students can easily click on it to get the most up-to-date information.

E-mail Policy: This is another area where it is best to check with your school to see if they have a college-wide policy. If not, check with your department. This policy should let students know what needs to be included in an e-mail, how you would like to be addressed, and any other requirements you might have. Let's start by talking about required information. Many instructors require students to include the class name and section number in the subject line. This is especially helpful if you teach multiple courses. It is also very important to let the students know how to address you. Do you have a title such as doctor that you want them to use? Or can they call you by your first name? If you do not tell them, they will not know. One other important aspect of your e-mail policy is to require all students to use their college-issued e-mail account. You, in turn, must use your college-issued e-mail account for all course related conversations.

Netiquette Policy: A netiquette policy helps to clarify expectations of online interaction. Most colleges and/or departments have developed a netiquette policy, so be sure to check on that. If the school cannot provide a policy for you, a quick Internet search will provide you with many examples. Having a clear netiquette policy for your class protects the students, you, and the interactions you create.

Required Technology Statement: Obviously, students who take an Internet class will be familiar with your LMS and have access to a computer and an Internet connection… or so you would think. It is not uncommon for a student without these things to be placed into an Internet class. It is important for you to be clear about the technology expectations for this class. This section needs to begin with the expectation of access to a computer and Internet and the ability to use your college's LMS. Other things you may want to include here might include:

- All software requirements such as any word processing software requirements, e-mail and publisher course pack software
- Any hardware requirements. Will students need a webcam? Microphone? Speakers?

Plagiarism Policy: Your college and/or department will have a plagiarism policy. Be sure to of sure either link to it or post it on your syllabus.

Student Code of Conduct Policy: This is another policy that it is important to link to.

Disclaimer: It is always wise to add a sentence on your syllabus stating that this syllabus is subject to change. We generally state something like this: "This syllabus may be subject to change as we move through this class." This is important in case a weather emergency or a leadership change, either of which that could cause changes to either your class schedule or course policies.

Course Schedule and Due Dates:
It is important to give students, especially online students, a clear picture of the due dates for work in the class. Online learners are often juggling many other things in life in addition to your class, so a clearly written schedule is critical for their success.

Other items that you may want to include:

- Other requirements: Does your class require an internship or other additional requirement? Be sure to include this information.
- Optional course materials: If there are any additional materials that students need to purchase for your class, you must list it on the syllabus. It is unfair to surprise students with additional expenses in the middle of the class.
- Message from the instructor: This is great way for you to give the students a little information about you, your teaching philosophy, and any other information that you would like to share. Students who make connections to you will be more comfortable reaching out and connecting with you and the course work in other ways, too.

Great Communication

◄ Phone students at the beginning of the course to answer any questions they may have.

◄ Be polite, open and responsive in communications you have with students.

◄ Give frequent and encouraging feedback.

◄ Be understanding and flexible.

◄ Privately congratulate individual students on good grades. Ask what happened when grades are lower than usual.

4.1 Course Development

When you first agree to develop an online course, it may not seem like a big undertaking. However, once you begin, it can quickly become overwhelming. It is easy to fall into a rut of being an information manager, not an instructor. However, online courses should be as engaging to the student as any seated course. The development of an online course will follow the same steps that the development of a seated course would take, with one important addition - all of the information exchanged will need to be done electronically.

◀ Training: Many colleges and schools have experts to help you navigate your LMS and to help with course development. Talk to your chair or coordinator to locate these resources and take advantage of them. A well developed course will result in higher rates of student success. If your school does not have these resources, inquire about working with a seasoned full time faculty member.

In today's technology driven world, it is more important than ever to understand how to use the tools contained in your school's LMS properly. This knowledge can be the difference between having a successful semester and not. Seek out training not only from your college, but also from the Internet. Most learning management systems have training resources on their websites, and YouTube is an excellent resource for training on specific actions and resources available within your LMS.

◀ Include Variety: Online students do well when they understand the flow of the course. For example, you may have your assignments due the same day of the week throughout the course, have the students complete a big test for every three chapters, or have the same basic types of assignments available for each unit. However you set up your course, it is important to have a rhythm to the work in your course that the students can easily understand and follow.

While it is important to have a rhythm to the workflow in your course, mix up the assignments or the specific goals within the assignments. Instead of having students complete the same type of activity over and over, give them some variety. For example, you might mix up the following assignments: worksheets, interactive websites, quizzes and case studies. Mixing up these type of assignments, keeps your course interesting and lets you assess mastery in various ways. This also benefits students who may struggle with one type of assignment, but excel at another. Resist the urge to include assignment types just to include them. Make sure you provide assignments and resources in the best formats for the learning goals you want to assess. For example, a multiple-choice practice quiz may not be the best way for students in a counseling skills course to show their knowledge, but instead a case study would be very effective.

◀ Accessibility: The Americans with Disabilities Act, and other accessibility guidelines and laws, require that all course content be accessible for all students. This requirement stands even if you do not have any students with disabilities in your course. Failure to do so will not only put your students at a disadvantage, but may also open your school to litigation. Most schools have a person or department tasked with helping faculty to create accessible material for their courses. Ask your department chair or coordinator for a referral to your college's resources.

In short, all of your course information should "provide multiple ways for students to gain knowledge, demonstrate knowledge, and interact" (Burgstahler, 2017). With changes in technology, what is considered compliant is constantly being redefined, so it is best to talk to an expert at your school to get the most up to date information. Accessibility leads us to using Universal Course Design.

◀ Universal Course Design: Using the principles of Universal Course Design is an important element in developing any course. Universal Course Design refers to using a variety of teaching methods to create course content and assess learning. Student diversity requires instructors create educational equity that allows students to learn using the tools and strategies that best meet their individual needs.

Universal Course Design also addresses accessibility. For example, when posting a video, make sure that there is a transcript or closed captioning available. When creating assignments, allow students to turn in the completed work in different formats. Instead of requiring a paper, you may decide to give students the option to create a video, presentation, or other option instead. It is important to hold students to the same standards of work while allowing for some flexibility in the finished product. This will not only allow your students to learn and show their learning in manners that show their strengths, it also gives you some variety in finished products to grade.

4.2 Storyboards

Creating a well laid out plan during course development will help you allocate your planning time effectively. In essence, then, a storyboard is a plan. A storyboard is especially useful as a kind of outline before designing a course in order to create clear navigation for students. A storyboard can be as simple as a flow chart, and it can feature only text, though the use of even rough illustrations will provide additional clarity.

The advantages of using a storyboard for planning rather than jumping right into site construction are several. First, storyboarding allows you to clarify goals for each part of your course and then to analyze the style and format in which you want to achieve those goals. Then, storyboarding helps you organize your material into modules and next to identify the online tools that your students will need. Finally, as you create the storyboard, problems will appear more obvious—don't they always on paper? You'll be able to identify and correct those problems more easily. This process can ultimately ease frustration so you don't feel overwhelmed and get lost in your own creation. *(The advice of course designers is to simplify. Limit the elements on any single screen so that scrolling is unnecessary; instead, break the information down into two or three linked screens.)*

The simplest way to start is to take the syllabus (yours or the department's) and figure out how you want its elements organized on your site. For example, some instructors release all materials right away, while others make sure that students demonstrate their proficiency before the next unit's material will be released to them. Some instructors place all PowerPoint presentations on one organizer page and all case studies on another. Other instructors might group materials according to topic, placing a PowerPoint presentation and a case study related to Enron on one organizer page, for example. The key is to plan and organize meticulously.

For more information, here are some links to storyboard templates:

◀ For those who like lists: https://deit.southwest.tn.edu/coe/resources/ExampleB/

◀ A detailed worksheet that leads you step-by-step through planning your online course: http://www.nottingham.ac.uk/elan/tutorials/How_do_I_start_to_storyboard

Here are links to some sample completed storyboards:

◀ A combination of text and flow chart that helps plan how an individual Web page will be laid out: http://www.ion.uillinois.edu/Resources/pointersclickers/2004_09/index.asp

◀ A flowchart in which each box describes one Web page: http://web.cortland.edu/flteach/mm-course/flowchart.html

◀ A graphical flow chart that uses symbols to represent each kind of course activity: https://venngage.com/blog/flow-chart-template/

◀ Storyboard apps: https://blog.hubspot.com/marketing/storyboard-software

4.3 Copyright Issues

Copyright laws related to distance education were clarified in 2002 with the passage of the Technology, Education and Copyright Harmonization Act (the TEACH Act), part of the Justice Department Reauthorization Act.

In general, original works, except those in the public domain, such as government works or those whose copyright has expired (usually seventy years after the author's death), are protected by copyright law and cannot be used except in very limited ways.

The provision in the new law to which you should pay special attention is that if you include copyrighted material under the "fair use" standard, you must abide by the following restrictions: If you allow students access to material, their access must be limited to a short time period and they must not be allowed to print or store that material in any way, even as a study tool at a later point. The limits on the time period for an online course are not specifically stated, but the safest course of action is to provide only temporary access to copyrighted material. Check with your distance education administrator about how to limit student access to parts of your site and how to disable print options for some material.

As for what constitutes fair use, that's debatable. If a work was published up through 1922, it's in the public domain and may be used freely. If a work was published between 1923 and 1978, it may or may not still have copyright protection. When a work is still under copyright, you need to evaluate whether your use is "fair" or whether you must seek permission to use the work. A good way to do this is to take the test at https://fairuse.stanford.edu/overview/fair-use/four-factors/, which asks you to decide where, on a scale, your purpose falls related to what kind of work it is; how you will use it; how much of it you will use; and what effect your use will have on the market for the original.

Remember also that you may not scan or upload full or lengthy works, and access to the course must be limited to enrolled students. In addition, you need to post a notice to students that materials used in connection with the course may be subject to copyright protection. (This note might instead be posted by the college on the distance learning main page.)

Even if you violate copyright laws out of ignorance, you are still liable. If found guilty, the fines for each act of "willful infringement" may be as high as $150,000.

An excellent overview called "Distance Education and the TEACH Act," is available at https://library.osu.edu/blogs/copyright/2015/06/12/navigating-the-teach-act-in-distance-education/.

4.4 Free Resources

The Web is rich with free resources for college instructors; the challenge is locating the sites. Here are a few sites created explicitly for higher education faculty for use in courses taught both online and offline. Adapt these ideas to fit your own teaching style. While it's not always explicitly stated on these sites, if you do borrow from any source, you should credit the creator.

◀ CAREO (Campus Alberta Repository of Educational Objects) is a Canadian project with 4,047 learning objects such as a chemistry lab, an interactive geometry tutorial and grammar games: http://www.careo.org/

◀ College and University Syllabi Published on the Internet The Open Syllabus Project offers syllabi in several dozen categories: http://opensyllabusproject.org/

◀ MERLOT-X, which stands for Multimedia Educational Resource for Learning and Online Teaching, offers over 10,000 Web-based learning materials created and constantly expanded by faculty across the country. Faculty members in fourteen disciplines contribute lesson plans, which are then peer reviewed and rated. Reviewers award up to five stars for course material, based on criteria in three categories: quality of content, potential effectiveness as a teaching-learning tool, and ease of use. It is maintained by the California State University Center for Distributed Learning: http://www.merlotx.org/find/modules.html

◀ MIT OpenCourseWare includes shareable course syllabi, assignments, and other resources for 701 courses at the Massachusetts Institute of Technology: https://ocw.mit.edu/index.htm

◀ Online Collections of Syllabi links to both general collections and field-specific collections of syllabi and is maintained by the American Academy of Religion in Atlanta, Georgia: https://www.aarweb.org/programs-services/syllabus-project

◀ Syllabus Finder contains over 500,000 syllabi from college courses and is maintained by the Center for History and New Media at George Mason University: https://www.syllabusfinder.com/

◀ World Lecture Hall has course materials for 1,550 courses in 83 categories submitted by professors around the world and is maintained by the Center for Instructional Technologies at the University of Texas at Austin: http://life.nthu.edu.tw/~g854205/lethall.htm

Chapter Five
STRATEGIES FOR TEACHING

5.1 Learning Styles

Attention to the way students learn is just as important in online courses as it is in the traditional classroom. Yet, while you may regularly design face-to-face activities that involve visual and audio components, group work, and physical movement, you may still be relying heavily on the written word when delivering courses online.

In the past, we often considered learning style theory to help us to understand how individuals process information. Learning style theory argued that individuals have a dominant learning style that directs how they will best learn new information. For example, the theory suggested that a student could be a "visual learner," "auditory learner," or "kinesthetic learner." The theory relied heavily on the work of Howard Gardner and his work on Multiple Intelligences (1993), wherein he identified eight intelligences that drive how we learn.

Figure 3: Multiple Intelligences

Howard Gardner proposed in his 1993 book Multiple Intelligences that people learn differently and that each of us is smart in at least one of seven ways:

◄ Linguistic intelligence (language)
◄ Logical-mathematical intelligence (numbers)
◄ Spatial intelligence (pictures)
◄ Bodily-kinesthetic intelligences (body)
◄ Musical intelligence (music)
◄ Interpersonal intelligence (people)
◄ Intrapersonal intelligence (self)
◄ Naturalist intelligence (nature)

Pedagogical research has shifted us away from the learning styles theory. The primary criticism of Gardner's research is that we are simply not as easily defined as learners as the theory would have us believe (Willingham et. al. 2015; Dekke et. al. 2012). Despite the intuitive nature of the theory, research does not support the idea that we can be neatly slotted into learning style categories. However, the theory has taught us one important lesson—students learn better when information is presented in multiple ways.

In the online learning environment, it is easy to rely on text-based materials. These certainly have their benefits, including availability, ease of integration into your courses and relevance to the course content. You are likely to have a textbook (either in print or ebook format), so continuing that type of content delivery is both easy and relevant. Yet, it is important to consider whether this is the best way to present material, or whether your text-based materials may need something additional.

The most common mistake made by faculty who are new to online learning is to underestimate the need for interaction and engagement with and among learners. This is manifested by a failure to include interaction, discussion, or feedback into every online assignment.

In addition to encouraging student interaction, you need to pay attention to the multiple ways that students take in information. For example, for each unit you could provide a trio of alternatives: a PowerPoint outline, transcripts of your lectures, and the lectures themselves streamed live or recorded and uploaded to a website like YouTube before being embedded into your course. Recorded lectures can be stopped and started as needed by the individual student and can provide a platform to embed review and critical thinking questions to actively engage the student in the learning process. Research suggests that students learn more deeply from words and visuals than from words alone, and multimedia presentations encourage active cognitive engagement and lead to more meaningful learning (Mayer 2003).

In contrast, inundating students with print materials can bore and overwhelm them. Richard Felder teaches chemical engineering at North Carolina State University, and writes regularly about distance education in his field. He presents a scenario that shows how an online course could engage a learner in multiple ways. In the example, the student reviews a multimedia tutorial that includes photos and diagrams and poses critical thinking questions, watches a video of the course instructor giving a lecture, retrieves information from a database to build an equation, exchanges e-mail with the instructor, and participates in a chat room with the other members of a team to discuss a joint project.

In short, when considering how to deliver course content and engage the students in learning activities, it is important to match the delivery method to the content being learned and provide multiple options for students to engage. Consider the information being presented and think about how you would present this information in a face-to-face class. With today's technology, the options for engaging, interactive, and meaningful learning experiences are broader than ever, and it is likely that you will be able to find a way to mimic face-to-face learning in the online classroom.

5.2 Accessibility

Since 1998, when Congress amended the Rehabilitation Act, federal agencies have been required under Section 508 of the law to make electronic and information technology accessible to those with disabilities. Coupled with the older and more inclusive Americans with Disabilities Act, there is a greater emphasis on creating online courses that can be accessed by everyone.

We discussed accessibility previously, but it bears repeated attention and is essential to consider when delivering your online course. To make your courses more accessible, post materials in different formats. For example, an assignment may be posted as a webpage and also in PDF format. A lecture may be posted as a text document and in PowerPoint outline form. Once you've been teaching online for awhile and have chosen to add more diverse resources to your course, go further. For instance, create HTML tags for illustrations to help the blind and avoid certain colors for those with color blindness. *Look at your entire course site and its ease of use from the perspective of those with disabilities.* Here are some free tools that can help:

- A list of the requirements for Section 508: https://www.access-board.gov/guidelines-and-standards/communications-and-it/about-the-section-508-standards/guide-to-the-section-508-standards
- Web Accessibility Initiative, a good overview: https://www.w3.org/WAI/Resources/
- Adobe offers information and tools to make PDF files accessible: https://www.adobe.com/accessibility/resources.html
- Microsoft offers tutorials for using accessibility features in Windows, Word, Outlook, and Internet Explorer: https://www.microsoft.com/en-us/accessibility/

- STEP508 is a tool for prioritizing Web site accessibility problems: https://www.section508.gov/index.php
- Toptal color blindness filter will show you how your page will look to someone who is colorblind: https://www.toptal.com/designers/colorfilter
- Understood is a great resource for Universal Design for Learning: https://www.understood.org/en/learning-attention-issues/treatments-approaches/educational-strategies/universal-design-for-learning-what-it-is-and-how-it-works
- Natural Reader screen reader software: https://www.naturalreaders.com/

If your institution has a distance learning department and/or an office of accessibility or disability services, it will be important for you to work with them to get help with accessibility in your course. All of the tools you use in your courses should also have accessibility statements, so look for those when you decide to add a tool and make sure the things you use are as accessible as possible. Be sure to check the closed captioning accuracy of any public videos that you include, and add captioning to videos that you produce yourself or provide a transcript if needed. Your distance learning professionals are likely to have good resources for making your course accessible, and they will be some of your best allies when designing your course.

Another excellent resource will be your librarians. Librarians are skilled researchers and will be excellent sources of accessible content for you to include. Reach out and make use of the people and resources offered by your institution to make sure each student enrolled in your course receives a quality learning experience.

5.3 Community Building

In teaching a distance education course you are, in a sense, building your own little community. You are not just the facilitator; you are the mayor. Your #1 goal is to keep the citizens from moving out.

Attrition rates for distance education programs have historically been higher than for traditional college courses, with dropout rates as high as 80 percent at some colleges, though this trend is changing as programs mature. Many of the reasons—such as students' inexperience with technology, or insufficient student support services—are beyond a faculty member's control. However, you can have a tremendous impact on student retention simply in the way you communicate. The form, frequency, promptness, and tone of written and oral interaction with students are very important.

The trick is to create a sense of classroom community. If students feel connected, if they believe that you have a personal interest in them, they will be less likely to drop out. This is often called "instructor immediacy." Immediacy refers to the idea that communication in the classroom is a key feature of the learning process. Verbal and nonverbal immediacy, through behaviors such as calling a student by name, using e-mail effectively, and using prosocial behaviors and language, have been shown to be strongly correlated with both cognitive and affective learning within the classroom (Baker, 2005).

Research by Angie Parker (2006), who teaches at Yavapai College, shows that those students with a higher "internal locus of control," or level of self-motivation, were more likely to complete a course. For students taking distance education courses, such an internal control was even more important, because these students must function more independently. This self-motivation is a learned trait, but it develops more readily through positive reinforcement; if students in online courses feel that they're alone as they struggle with the technology as well as the course material, they are in greater danger of dropping out. In distance education, Parker concludes, "Instructional intervention can be a powerful tool for accelerating motivational change."

The dramatic increase in the number of online courses at colleges and universities—and the problem of hanging on to students unprepared for this new way of learning—are leading to some research efforts aimed at systematically examining both issues. "Quality on the Line: Benchmarks for Success in Internet-Based Distance Education" (2000), a study by the Institute for Higher Education Policy, recommends that contact between faculty and students be "facilitated through a variety of ways, including voice-mail and/or e-mail" and that "Feedback to student assignments and questions is constructive and provided in a timely manner." Communication is key, the study concludes.

In discussing community online, Dr. Gary Wheeler (Wheeler, 2003) quotes a study by Palloff and Pratt that defines the basic steps for establishing a virtual community. The steps are:

◄ Clearly define the purpose of the group

◄ Create a distinctive gathering place for the group

◄ Promote effective leadership within the group

‹ Define norms and a clear code of conduct

‹ Allow for a range of member roles

‹ Allow for and facilitate subgroups

‹ Allow members to resolve their own disputes.

Allowing students to resolve their own conflicts results in improved communication within the group. Since face-to-face interchange is not possible, online discussions in which students present conflicting viewpoints introduce a degree of emotion into the learning process. However, you must be careful to monitor the discussions so that they don't deteriorate into personal conflicts and discourage dialogue.

One way to do this to set a positive tone from the start: be personal, polite, open and responsive in communications you have with individual students, and with the class as a whole. When responding to students' questions and comments on the discussion board and in e-mail, always use their names. Make frequent use of terms like "please" and "thanks." Be sure to watch your wording so it is as positive as possible. For example, instead of saying that a student has done something incorrectly and leaving it at that, include targeted feedback with wording that lets them know how to improve for the next assignment and ensures them that you believe they are capable of the improvement. All of this takes extra time, but it's worth it.

It's a good idea to keep most communication within a course, such as on a discussion board, so you don't end up repeatedly answering the same question. E-mail can also be a great tool for personal encouragement and for friendly reminders about assignments that are upcoming or overdue. *Keep students on task by sending weekly e-mails to those who did not post on the discussion board to let them know their contributions were missed. Many learning management systems automate these types of messages, and include tools to help with reminders.* For example, Remind (www.remind.com) is a free tool that sends text messages to your students without revealing your personal phone number. You can schedule reminders before your course starts that can be sent later to give students a reminder of upcoming due dates. You can then use it as a quick message tool to contact students individually or in groups while maintaining your own phone privacy.

Another way to encourage communication is to make yourself available at times and in a manner that is most helpful for students. This doesn't mean that you need to chain yourself to your computer 24/7, but it might mean that you hold a targeted online office hour one day or evening a week for the students in your online course, perhaps the night before an assignment is due. Make it easy for students to contact you instantly, either in a chat room through the courseware or via an instant messaging tool such as Google Hangouts, Remind, or Facebook Messenger.

Here are some practical tips for fostering good communication in online courses:

◄ Introduce Yourself. Make sure your students know who is teaching the class. Add a photo and bio, link to a website bio that you have created, or create an introduction video. When students see that there is an actual person behind the course, they will know that you are more engaged. If your learning management system allows for it, post a picture as your avatar, and encourage your students to do so as well. It is much more inviting when communication occurs with someone you can see, even if it's through a picture.

◄ Build a learning community. Have students post written introductions (and photographs if possible) on the discussion board—and post one yourself. Encourage students to interact with discussions about course material, either through a space on your site or in temporary chat rooms. Create an area online for socializing.

◄ Give frequent and encouraging feedback. You might adapt the practices of a biology instructor at Piedmont Technical College in Greenwood, South Carolina, who holds online office hours, responds to e-mail within 24 hours, gives a range of dates for an exam to be completed, and responds to students individually with their grades and where they stand in the course.

◄ Maximize the use of the discussion board to encourage group interaction. Minimize the use of e-mail for communication, and keep communication on the discussion board as much as possible. Encourage students to answer each other's questions.

◄ Check in daily to answer questions and redirect discussions if they get off track. Students need to sense your presence, though you don't want to intrude. Some instructors post on discussion boards a few times during the week while others write a weekly posting which comments directly on what students have had to say during the week. Even if a problem seems to be developing, hold back for a little while, for often the group will resolve its own conflicts and be stronger for it. But if discussions veer wildly off track, post a follow-up question to help recapture the focus. If you don't have discussion boards, this can be done through an announcements forum or group e-mail.

◀ Be encouraging, understanding, and flexible. Congratulate students on a good effort. Ask what happened when a grade was low or they missed an assignment. Allow them some time flexibility in completing assignments, if possible, by creating a reasonable time frame for submission. Share a little of yourself. Reach out to students who are struggling. A simple note to a student asking, "Is everything OK? I haven't heard from you in a while," can give a student under great pressure the reassurance that someone cares.

◀ Make class fun. Bramucci (2001) offers many ideas for inject-ing an impish spirit and for giving students reasons to check into the class more often. For example, he suggests a weekly "Guess who?" feature based on unusual facts gathered by the teacher about each student. "Hide" actual test questions on the site in a sort of "Where's Waldo?" activity. Post teasers about interesting information to be covered in an upcoming lesson. Post holiday greetings. Invite students to submit nominations for a joke of the week. Send a Friday greeting with wishes for a good weekend.

◀ Use an Icebreaker. Maybe more so than with a class taught face-to-face, an icebreaker can be an asset for distance education courses. It commences communication immediately, gives the students a chance to participate and use the technology, and gives the instructor an opportunity to observe student writing styles.

Chapter Six

VIRTUAL CLASSROOM TECHNIQUES

6.1 Text Lectures

You wouldn't think of spending a class period reading to your students in a monotone from lecture notes that summarize a homework reading assignment. Nevertheless, when it comes to online lectures, that same care is sometimes not applied. Lectures must capture students' interest without undermining the reading and work that you had them complete before coming to class.

If you lack the time to craft an illuminating written lecture for each section of your online courses, you may be tempted to resort to posting lecture notes to your LMS hoping that the notes will help students understand the material. However, in doing so, you cheat your online students out of important materials you routinely deliver to your face-to-face students: your sense of humor, your memorable anecdotes to highlight factual information and your passion for the subject.

Online lectures offer a slightly different challenge. However, with a little planning, the online lecture experience can be just as rich for your students as it will be for you.

Here are some tips to improve your online lectures:

1. Start small. Begin with one lecture for one topic in one class. Otherwise, the prospect of writing dozens of lectures could overwhelm you.

2. Keep it short. It's easy for online lectures to ramble, with links to subtopics that sometimes lead to even more sub-subtopics. Making such information available to students is a good idea, but post these links separately, and limit the lecture to about 1000 words or no more than 5 minutes (or a maximum of 15 minutes). This will help keep students engaged.

3. Make it personal. Online lectures should convey a sense of the instructor's personality. While certain subjects lend themselves to personal reflections more than others, every good teacher ventures at least an opinion, if not a personal story, during a lecture.

4. Write in a conversational style. Write it the way you would say it. If you use humor or jokes, be sure to keep them in there.

5. Draw connections to everyday things. As you know, comparing new ideas to what students already understand fosters learning.

6.2 Audio and Video Lectures

Audio

Presentations you've been using in the classroom can be brought to life online by adding an audio narrative. This format is great for material that is graphical in nature—such as illustrations, charts, and diagrams—and which would benefit from elaboration. Podcasts are popular with many students. This is an audio version of something like a quick lecture. It allows students to listen to the information without being tied to a screen. You may also consider providing an audio recording of you delivering the lecture that you have also provided in text format. The dual presentation of the material offers choice and multiple avenues for understanding for your students.

Video

There are many professionally-made videos on a variety of topics available on the Internet that you can link directly to your course. There are also many of lower quality, though, so be careful what you use. Video providers such as Khan Academy, TED, and Crash Course create some of the most commonly used high quality videos. Other sources, such as OpenStax, a provider of open resource textbooks, have created quality resources with the help of faculty who use their books. As a general rule, when planning your first online course, consider "finding" before "making" if you are in a time crunch to create your course, but make one of your first ongoing goals for your course delivery be to create your own video lectures. Having your own lectures ensures they are relevant and targeted specifically toward the material you are covering.

Creating both videos and audio lectures will require you to decide which software program you want to use. It is best to touch base with you chair to determine if the college uses a specific program. If they do not and you are allowed to select a software program yourself, spend some time investigating the many that are available online. One thing to keep in mind is that you will need to make sure that it is compatible with your LMS. Some learning management systems have built-in resources for recording lectures, as do many publisher resource sites. Other instructors may choose to upload videos to YouTube, which can allow you to either post a link in your course or potentially embed the video directly into your course site.

Most experts recommend that you limit each lecture to about 5-15 minutes, since online learning often happens in small chunks of time. This allows students to stop, start and replay parts of the lecture as necessary. For variety, you can bring in guest speakers, or use humor or surprising graphics. For example, record a conversation between you and a colleague on a topic, organize and film a short panel discussion, interview experts, or give a demonstration.

Many boring video lectures are available online. Before making your own video lecture, conduct a Web search to see for yourself how boring some video lectures can be. You will quickly note that many of the worst offenders have simply filmed themselves giving a lecture; the "talking head" approach is deadly dull. A quick search on YouTube will yield 45-60 minute videos of a professor lecturing in the front of an auditorium classroom without the benefit of seeing the slides or demonstrations that are happening off camera. Instead, consider other approaches. I recently helped a colleague who was teaching British Literature help the students grasp the cultural climate of the British 18th century. We each donned fancy hats and time period clothing and had a "tea party," where we discussed our lives. The result was hilarious and memorable.

It is also fun to invite the students to create short videos on selected topics. Most students today have smart phones that will allow them to upload contact directly to YouTube and your LMS. This can be especially interesting in a discussion board format. It can also be something that you assign to a different group of or individual students for each chapter, module, or unit to engage them and help them to both review the material for themselves and help their classmates to understand it more fully.

6.3 Discussions

No matter what the subject area, well-run discussions create a sense of community in online courses. It is also easy to turn discussions into drudgery for both the students and instructor. The trick is to create discussion questions that encourage critical thinking, and then to follow up students' responses with questions that encourage them to think ever more deeply about the topic. One way to do this is to pose

Figure 4: Bloom's Taxonomy

Use Bloom's Taxonomy to create more difficult questions as the term progresses:

Knowledge (ask questions that begin with words like list, define, tell, describe, identify, show, label, examine, tabulate, quote, name)

Comprehension (ask questions that begin with words like summarize, describe, interpret, contrast, predict, associate, distinguish, estimate, differentiate, discuss, extend)

Application (ask questions that begin with words like apply, demonstrate, calculate, complete, illustrate, show, solve, examine, relate)

Analysis (ask questions that begin with words like analyze, separate, order, explain, connect, classify, arrange, divide, compare, select, explain, infer)

Synthesis (ask questions that begin with words like combine, integrate, modify, rearrange, substitute, plan, create, design, invent, compose, formulate, prepare, generalize, rewrite)

Evaluation (ask questions that begin with words like assess, decide, rank, grade, test, measure, recommend, convince, select, judge, explain, discriminate, support, conclude, compare, summarize)

your questions according to Bloom's Taxonomy, which ranks thinking in six increasingly sophisticated levels. In terms of discussion topics, you want springboards that are complex, perhaps controversial, and relevant in terms of the content and the students' interests and experiences.

Here are some examples of potentially rich types of discussion topics:

◀ Current events: Connect an issue of widespread interest to course material. For example, the debate about whether to restrict immigration would offer a good starting point for discussion about the immigrant narratives students were reading in American literature.

◄ Controversy: Make a current controversy the topic of a debate. A biology class might debate whether stem cell research should be allowed; a criminal justice class might tackle the use of tasers by police officers. If you use a controversial topic, be sure to monitor the discussion closely.

◄ Role play: Give a hypothetical situation, and ask different students to assume roles in the discussion. An education class might assume roles of parents, students, administrators, and school board members engaged in a discussion of the merits of instituting a new dress code policy or a year-round school calendar.

◄ What if?: Offer students a fantasy question that encourages a creative approach to the material. For example, ask literature students to imagine how three specific characters would react if thrown together in a lifeboat, or what might happen after the end of another story. One of my favorite class discussions asks students what three brain structures they would give up in a ridiculous hypothetical experiment, which they would definitely keep, and why they would choose them. While fun for them, it also requires them to explain brain anatomy and physiology and keeps the discussion lively.

◄ Statistical analysis: Give some interesting facts and ask students to analyze them. For example, using the Statistical Abstract of the United States, an economics class might look at the U.S. population and talk about the ramifications of the large number of Baby Boomers reaching retirement age.

◄ Exemplification: Ask students to provide examples from the reading or from their own experience to illustrate a concept. For example, teach grammar by calling on students to write sentences illustrating particular rules.

◄ Case study: Post a case study and ask for analysis. In a business communications class, students might receive a scenario about an employer having problems with excessive employee absences during the summer, which was his busy season. They would discuss possible solutions to the problem.

Once students have posted their replies to the topic, follow up with questions. You should look to Bloom's Taxonomy for terms to use within your questions that will encourage the students reach higher levels of understanding. Muilenburg and Berge (2004), citing earlier research by L.B. Savage, offer these examples of probing follow-ups:

◄ What reasons do you have for saying that?

◄ Why do you agree (or disagree) on that point?

◄ How are you defining the term that you just used?

◄ What do you mean by that expression?

◄ Is what you are saying here consistent with what you said earlier?

◄ Could you clarify that remark?

◄ When you say that, what is implied by your remarks?

◄ What could follow from what you just said?

◄ Is it possible you and he are contradicting each other?

◄ Are you sure you're not contradicting yourself?

◄ What alternatives are there to such a formulation?

A course with many students and with active discussions can quickly become time consuming. To keep the workload manageable, remember that while it's important for the instructor to participate, you don't have to—and shouldn't—respond to every posting or to every student. In fact, doing so prevents students from taking ownership of the information; they reply less often to each other, and rarely look to one another for insight.

You can get students even more involved, and save yourself some work, if you make them individually, or in groups, responsible for some of the discussion topics; they can post the topic, respond occasionally to foster further discussion, and post a summary once the discussion is over.

To keep the discussion board organized, create distinct threads for different topics. Use separate threads or separate discussion forums for questions and announcements. You may also want to create a thread or forum just for personal exchanges, a kind of student lounge where they might share accomplishments and commiserate over disappointments. Another option is to create an anonymous thread, where students can feel uninhibited about posting concerns about the course.

To ensure participation, discussion postings must be required. Make clear how often students must post, and give them specific guidelines about the quantity and quality (along with a model) of an acceptable response to the topic. You should also model such responses through your own postings.

To ensure interaction, you may want to require that students reply to a minimum number of classmates per topic or per week. Students especially need guidelines on these replies so that the discussion doesn't consist of postings like "good comment" or "I agree." They need help in understanding how to add specific information that expands and deepens the discussion. Encourage them to respectfully disagree with one another, since debates make for the most interesting discussion, and encourage them to offer personal anecdotes that illustrate the discussion topic; for example, in a class in which students read some nonfiction about racism, several students wrote about experiences in which they felt they had been mistreated because of their race.

To help students become proficient at this kind of interaction, post a model interaction, and model such replies yourself. Reply to some of the student comments applauding specifically what was so good, and for the first few weekly summaries, include examples of excellent replies. To get students to read carefully, and to value their classmates' postings, you might require that in one of their papers, students must refer specifically to (and document) a classmate's posting relevant to their topic.

A few more tips:

◀ **Deadlines:** Set rigid deadlines. Use weekly topics, with no credit for postings once the week ends, no matter what the reason. (To allow for unavoidable crises that will arise, however, late in the semester you might offer everyone an extra credit assignment equal in value to the grade for one week's postings or choose to drop the lowest discussion grade.)

◀ **Informality:** Make clear that while an error free posting is easier to read, students need not worry excessively about grammar, spelling and punctuation for discussion board postings unless that is a key aspect of the discussion itself. The discussion board is a place to explore ideas more informally while other assignments require higher standards of perfection.

◀ **Summary:** Post a summary at the end of a discussion topic to provide closure and to reinforce what was learned. Praise some of the most insightful postings.

◀ **Ascending complexity:** Structure discussion questions to make them more challenging as the term progresses.

6.4 Live Chats

While most aspects of online courses are asynchronous, with students working independently at times convenient for them, some research indicates that synchronous communication can be beneficial in the online environment (Moser and Smith, 2015). Synchronous meetings can help to remove the "distance" in distance education and can allow the for the exchange of ideas, explanations, and feedback. These sessions can also be used for review of materials before a test or as a mini-writing workshop. Most learning management systems have chat functionality built in, but there are other options such as Skype, Google Hangouts, or Zoom.

The problem with live chats is scheduling them and making sure students understand when they are required. This should be considered strongly when choosing to incorporate a synchronous element like a live chat into an asynchronous course. Some institutions, such as Kaplan College, have made weekly hour-long chats a course requirement. Students sign up for a class that has a chat session that fits their schedule. If you teach at an institution which doesn't have a chat requirement, though, it may be a challenge to find a chat time that suits everyone. To get around that obstacle, you can schedule multiple chats on the same topic. This allows students to find the time that works best for them. Another alternative is to schedule several chats on different topics and at different times throughout the term and to require that students attend a certain number (perhaps half) of them. Conversely, you can make the chats optional, though attendance likely will not be high in that case. Another option is to hold several chats at different times during the semester. Require attendance at all, but offer students unable to participate the option of summarizing the session from a transcript.

Chat tips:

◀ An ideal online chat session will last 60 minutes—long enough to cover one or more topics in some depth.

◀ Note the days and times when your students tend to be online, and schedule a chat at that time.

◀ Limit the number of students in the chat. 10-12 would be best, otherwise things can get confusing.

◄ Before the chat session begins, open documents that you want to post during the chat, and keep them minimized on your desktop for quick access. Since these sessions move so quickly, you'll want something you can quickly copy and paste into the chat room.

◄ Post chat transcripts so those who can't attend will benefit.

6.5 Guest Experts

Even online, the voice of a single course instructor can grow wearisome over the length of a semester. One way to hold student interest, and invigorate your own teaching, is to invite guest experts to interact with your class via discussion boards or chat rooms. The Internet makes it easier for guest experts to participate from any location. Ask guests to respond online to student comments over several days at their convenience. Guests may find such a request easier to grant than delivering a presentation during your on-campus class meeting. However, the process of arranging for guests and helping them to prepare can be involved.

When thinking of a person to invite into your class, consider your audience (the students). Invite a person with relevant knowledge who will hold students' attention. One obvious source is other faculty on your campus. Manufacturers and publishers would probably be delighted for the promotional opportunity. Community leaders or agency representatives are other great resources.

If you are not comfortable inviting someone in to talk with your class, look online for videos prepared by experts. TED Talks have a variety of short videos that work well in the online environment.

6.6 Real-Time Data Assignments

Real-time data, widely available online for subjects ranging from earthquake and hurricane activity to computer industry returns, offer you a dynamic source of information which changes frequently, sometimes hourly.

In economics courses at North Carolina State University in Raleigh, N.C., students try to predict who will win an election, whether the Federal Reserve is going to raise interest rates at its next meeting, or what the box office receipts of a movie are going to be in its first four weeks of release. Using real-time data web sites such as the Iowa Electronics Market, students make weekly virtual trades, then report on their reasoning as well as the outcomes of their decisions. With movies, for example, students try to develop a statistical model to predict box office returns. Based on such factors as the appeal of pre-release trailers and the star power of the leading actors, as well as the overall economy, they decide which film contracts would be the best buys.

The availability of real-time data makes course material much more immediate to the students. A biology class at Paradise Valley Community College in Phoenix, Arizona, uses data related to El Nino, hurricanes, temperatures, ozone, ocean currents, and state streams and rivers. At Georgia Perimeter College in Clarkston, Georgia, a geology instructor sends students online to check worldwide volcano activity. Students select a volcano to track, often picking based on some personal connection, such as travel experience, or relatives living near the site. Then they answer questions about the character of the eruption, the type of volcano and lava, the kinds of rocks forming from it, and how the volcano affects people living in the area. Students supplement their research with news reports, official government warnings, and information from volcano observatories and volcano-monitoring agencies, such as the U.S. Geological Survey.

Given the vast amount of information you can find online, you might use this as an optional assignment. Be sure to have a back-up site in case the real-time data suddenly become static (such as temperatures that might not produce very dramatic highs and lows when the weather has turned cloudy).

Here are some real-time data Web sites to get you started:

◀ El Nino information: https://www.climate.gov/enso

◀ National Oceanic and Atmospheric Administration: https://www.noaa.gov/

◀ National Earthquake Information Center: https://earthquake.usgs.gov/index.php

◀ National Hurricane Center: https://www.nhc.noaa.gov/

◀ Ozone data: https://airnow.gov/

◀ U.S. earthquakes: https://earthquake.usgs.gov/earthquakes/map/

◀ National Water Information System: https://waterdata.usgs.gov/nwis/

◀ Volcanoes: https://volcanoes.usgs.gov/index.html

6.7 Virtual Field Trips

The best educational websites, which involve students in a way that helps them become producers of knowledge, make for great virtual field trips.

The world of virtual reality is one of the areas that is rapidly growing at this time. Using virtual reality (VR), you can immerse your students in real life situations to allow them to engage in experiential learning. Students can tour historical sites, be part of surgery or experience old age. Students can purchase VR goggles for a few dollars. These VR goggles could be considered a required classroom supply on the syllabus. An online search will give you an idea of the variety and richness of VR resources available for free.

Here are some destinations where you might send your students:

◄ Geology field trips at https://www.e-education.psu.edu/geosc10/node/1802 take geology students on virtual field trips of the U.S. national parks.

◄ The Tempe, Arizona, Police Department Crime Unit at https://www.tempe.gov/government/police/crime-statistics-reports offers information about crime analysis, as well as crime statistics and trends. Michael Turturice, who teaches a criminal justice class at Tempe's McClintock High School, sends students to this site for information about crime in their own neighborhoods. (More innovative ideas can be found at http://www.vickiblackwell.com/vft.html)

◄ Multiple historic points of view related to the Civil War's Battle of Antietam can be contrasted at https://www.nps.gov/civilwar/multimedia.htm. These include visuals (photographs of the battlefield and monuments), eyewitness accounts, timelines, and military analysis. High school social studies teacher Kelly Fortner uses this and related sites to push students toward narrative and analytical projects. (See more of her ideas at http://lessonplanspage.com/sscicivilwarvirtualfieldtripplushyperstudiopres59.htm/)

◄ An online tour of The Holocaust Museum at https://www.ushmm.org/ allows visitors to move and examine artifacts, much as an on-site visitor might do. For example, if you choose to follow the links related to Suse Grunbaum, you'll see a photo of the cookbook she kept as a safer alternative to a diary and a photo of her in front of the hiding place under the floorboards of a barn where she and her family stayed for two years.

◀ The Mount Vernon tour at https://www.mountvernon.org/site/virtual-tour/ takes visitors through George Washington's mansion in a systematic manner—from floor plans to individual rooms to individual objects in each room. Accompanying each object is an explanation, often a quotation from Washington himself. This tour could work for an exercise in place description in a composition class or as a complement to classes in architecture or American history.

◀ The National Women's History Museum at https://www.womenshistory.org/ is helpful for visual reinforcement when American literature students read the *Declaration of Sentiments*. They can examine gold suffrage ribbons and suffrage playing cards (featuring a blindfolded American goddess of justice), and they can also test their knowledge about the early women's movement with a short quiz that asks such questions as "Why were some suffragists jailed?" Answer: for picketing the White House.

◀ Sites with frequently updated data are among the most fun. For example, an astronomy instructor might like to have students check their inspection of the night sky by visiting the Worchester, Massachusetts EcoTarium's virtual planetarium at https://ecotarium.org/event/planetarium-show/all/, which charts each night's visible stars and planets.

◀ The Exploratorium at https://www.exploratorium.edu/ is a treat of a different sort. You can learn about step dancing by moving different steps into a sequence of your choice and then viewing the resulting video. You can see how the hunting bow transformed—re-enacted before your eyes—into a Brazilian musical instrument called the berimbau. And you can learn how to forecast surfing conditions at the beach.

◀ The Rock and Roll Hall of Fame Museum is a great resource for lesson plans that use music. At https://www.rockhall.com/learn are ideas for using rock to teach economics, history, critical thinking, literary analysis, composition—and even music.

◄ For a good starting point, check out https://museums.fandom.com/wiki/Virtual_Library_museums_pages, with links to hundreds of online museums from around the globe.

6.8 Problem-Based Learning/Case Studies

Case studies and problem-based learning (PBL) have long been regular features of courses in law, medicine, and business. Now they are also gaining popularity as teaching tools for humanizing science, and for helping students think critically as they work their way through the scientific method in solving a problem. In addition, case studies are a great way for faculty who teach online to encourage critical thinking and to incorporate discussions, writing assignments, and group projects, excellent complements to fact-based web presentation of material. PBL offers real-world cases to students, who can work individually or in teams, to unravel the problems.

There are many excellent resources available online to locate case studies. Some publishers provide them, making them particularly relevant to the text you are using. Others can be found on websites and open resource databases. When selecting topics for case studies, be sure to select ones that are both interesting and relevant.

Here are a few examples, along with the name of the educator who wrote each one:

◄ Anatomy & Physiology: Use forensics to identify the sex, age, and height of a skeleton. (*Alease Bruce*, University of Massachusetts at Lowell)

◄ Chemistry: How safe are polycarbonate baby bottles? (*Michael A. Jeannot*, St. Cloud State University)

◄ Ecology: Who should manage the St. Croix River? (*Pamela Locke Davis*, University of Minnesota)

◄ Geology: What are the ethics involved in publicizing scientific discoveries too quickly, such as NASA's 1996 announcement that life existed on Mars? (*Bruce C. Allen and Clyde F. Herreid*, University at Buffalo)

◄ Physics: Use Newtonian mechanics to figure out how a cheerleader can lift up a 300-pound football player. (*Malati Patil*, University at Buffalo, State University of New York).

When using the case-study method, be sure that each case uses dialogue to tell a good story and that it's relevant, contentious, recent, and short.

6.9 Online Labs

In virtual science labs, students can handle dangerous poisons, analyze raging rivers, and conduct experiments in evolution. In virtual psychology labs, students can train a rat using the practices of classical and operant conditioning, or raise a child using the principles of human development. In math labs, students can practice skills and apply them to real-world problems. As technology continues to grow, these type of virtual experiments and activities are becoming more commonplace. There are websites that allow students to explore a brain, dissect body parts, and fly airplanes. As these experiences become more refined, they are being adopted in increasing numbers for online instruction.

Again, this is an area that is rapidly being developed, so take a little time to search the Internet for the most up to date creations. Consider the use of virtual or augmented reality software when possible as well. For example, using virtual reality goggles and appropriate software, students can take a walk through a Medieval village or travel through the brain.

Some colleges allow students to "check out" lab kits for science courses. Students have the use of a kit provided by the college for the semester that they are enrolled in that course. The kit provides the materials that they need to conduct the required labs for the course.

Allowing for these lab experiences to be conducted asynchronously is a way to add order to the chaos that results when fifteen lab students coming from different experiments have questions at the same time.

6.10 Games

Using simple games in an online course can offer variety and appeals to the natural pleasure most of us feel when playing a game. In short, games offer a different and particularly effective way to involve students. Games can be used as a kind of self-test for review. As a rule, educational games need to have rules, goals and objectives, outcomes and feedback. Some of the most popular kinds of simple games are crosswords and matching, as well as games modeled after popular TV shows such as *Jeopardy*.

A number of sites offer free versions of their game software that you can incorporate into your site:

◀ Hot Potatoes, free for educators, allows you to create six kinds of games, including crosswords and matching: https://hotpot.uvic.ca/

◀ Crossword Compiler: https://www.crossword-compiler.com

◀ QuizMaster: nine games, including Sink the Fleet and TicTacToe: http://cybertrain.info/quizman/qmselect.html

◀ Template for creating Jeopardy: https://jeopardylabs.com/

◀ Gamemaker, which includes a free version, allows you to design more complex games: http://www.yoyogames.com/make

◀ Matching Puzzle: five free games including crossword, hangman, slider puzzle, word search and memory squares: http://janmulder.com/

◀ Eclipse Crossword: https://www.eclipsecrossword.com/

◀ WebAuthor, a tool to create exercises for foreign language instruction: http://ccat.sas.upenn.edu/plc/larrc/webauthor.html

◀ Quiz Center, which hosts your games on its Web site: https://www.discoveryeducation.com/

◀ Form Builder, free for educators, which allows you to create simple quizzes: https://try.typeform.com

◀ Quizlet: includes a number of different game formats to help with review: https://quizlet.com/

6.11 Cooperative Assignments

Cooperative assignments for distance learning courses should be formatted in much the same manner as those given to students in face-to-face courses. You should structure the groups with several things in mind: all students must participate, you must develop a method to capture individual student participation, and a written product must be the result. As the facilitator, you must contribute through planning and total commitment. If they're handled well, online projects can mirror the real types of online collaboration that today's students will face in their careers.

One example of successful online collaboration among students is an online MBA course at Morehead State University in Morehead, Kentucky. Students choose an article from *Fast Company* magazine, post related discussion questions, and then summarize their class-mates' responses. They get together in a live chat area provided by the courseware, and also correspond via e-mail. Another group project they complete is an online press conference, in which half the group represents the media and the other half poses as a company's business managers. For about an hour in the group chat area, they engage in a question and answer session. These students also write case studies of business-related problems using both e-mail and an online drop box where students can exchange documents.

Group activities such as those outlined above work well thanks to "virtual team-building" exercises conducted early in the semester. In these exercises, students discuss group roles, and each student is urged to take on a task, such as taking notes at group meetings or e-mailing meeting reminders to each member. At the end of each group activity, feedback is elicited on the value of the project.

The peer review is another example of group work. Students post essay drafts for evaluation by classmates, according to guidelines set forth by the instructor.

Group projects increase interaction among students, but place demands upon students' out of class time. It is important to consider the busy lives of your students. Do not make this type of group as-signment one that takes more time than it is worth. Many students take online courses so that they can work independently on their own time.

Here are a few tips for facilitating effective group work:

◀ Roles: Require each team member to take on a role.

◀ Charter: Get the group to create a team charter, which spells out the expectations of group members, as well as guidelines for how they will communicate and how they'll handle conflict.

◀ Transparency: Insist that all communication be posted on a group discussion board. If the team uses a chat room for live discussion, have them post a transcript on the discussion board.

◀ Feedback: Allow each group member to evaluate his or her teammates at the conclusion of the project. You may or may not include that as a part of the individual's grade.

Chapter Seven

ASSESSMENT

7.1 Types of Assessment

When assessing student learning, the first task to consider is what type of assessment you need to do: formative or summative. Do you need to know if students are on the right track (formative), or do you need to know if they have met the learning objectives of your module, unit or course (summative)? Discussions about assessment in distance learning frequently focus on summative assessment, assessing the acquisition of knowledge at the end of a chapter, unit, or the whole course. *Remember that formative assessments are just as important in online courses as they are in the face-to-face classroom. In all of our courses, we need to do informal assessments along the way, even if it's just checking in at the end of class to find out if students have questions.* These are formative assessments. A comprehensive look at formative and summative assessments may be found in *Blended Learning and Flipped Classrooms* (Adams, Gingras, 2018):

Formative assessment is part of the instructional process. It is a tool to monitor student learning and to provide important feedback to the student. Formative assessment has two critical functions. First, it allows the students to identify their weaknesses and helps them to determine what areas on which they need additional work. Second, it allows you to identify problem areas in your teaching and course materials so you can adjust them. Formative assessments should have some bearing on the course grade, but should generally be treated as low-stakes with a lower point value and used as the learning is happening.

Summative assessment is used to measure the knowledge gained by your students at certain times in the course, such as when finishing a unit of work at or the end of the course. This measure is compared to a benchmark or standard, which is often set by your institution. Compared to formative assessment, summative assessment tends to have much higher stakes and higher point values.

Summative assessment is a measure, and not necessarily a learning tool, whereas formative assessment is used more as a learning tool.

When designing your online course, it is important to consider both formative and summative assessment techniques. Students need to know if they are on the right and have an opportunity to change things before they are ultimately assessed on their learning. It is also important to consider your assessments carefully, and choose assessment measures that best fit the material you are teaching.
. Here are some options:

- Ungraded quizzes and surveys for student self-assessment

- Multiple choice

- Matching

- True false

- Sequencing

- Fill in the blank

- Short answer

- Essay

- Portfolios

- Projects

- Papers and reports

- Group assignments

- Presentations

- Journal

- Problem solving

To help students prepare, post sample exams and sample responses— use previous student exams after you have secured permission from the students for such use. Provide both above average and below average student responses, along with commentary explaining the strengths and weaknesses of the various responses.

7.2 Formative Assessment

Formative learning assessments help gauge how well students are learning the material. Informal and sometimes ungraded, they solicit specific information about what students do and don't know while the learning is happening. They can let both you and the student know whether more resources, more discussion or more focus on a particular topic are needed. They can also be good sources of feedback on the organization and content of your course by letting you know whether you have allowed enough time, provided the right kinds of learning activities, and given enough of the right resources to your students. Though formative assessments are a bit harder to administer to online students than to students sitting in a classroom, getting this sort of feedback in a distance education class is even more valuable. Here are some options to consider:

- **Background Knowledge Probe**: At the beginning of the term, give students a list of terms related to the course, and ask them to rate their level of familiarity with each one.

- **Muddiest Point**: At the end of a lesson, ask students to name something they still don't understand. This can be done easily with a discussion board where students can be encouraged to help each other to understand the material as well as receive instructor help.

- **Classroom Polls**: Ask students what they like and don't like about the class or material so far, how confident they are in their learning or their attitudes about a particular issue within the unit or module.

- **Lessons**: Organizing the learning material into lessons, using something like SoftChalk (https://softchalk.com/) or a lesson resource within your learning management system can allow you to add small assessments within the material itself. For example, you can add quick quiz questions at different points in the lesson or add a muddiest point feedback option within the lesson itself. Not only will this give you a gradable form of low stakes assessment, but it will also keep the student engaged as they progress through the lesson.

- **Reading Notes**: Having students submit copies of their notes, perhaps within a template that can later serve as their study guide, can be a valuable assessment of study behaviors as well as learning.

- **Discussion Boards**: The standard formative assessment measure in online courses for years, discussion boards continue to be potentially valuable tools. You can design these to be muddiest point forums, reflections, or even a place to ask questions or create test questions.

- **Blogs/Journals**: Having students keep a blog or journal is a good way to monitor their progress to the material. Common ways to use blogs include reflections and linking learned material to "real life" applications.

- **Interactive Multimedia Presentations**: Publishers often have these available through their online resources, many can be found on the Internet, and it is increasingly easy to create these yourself. Tools such as Edpuzzle (https://edpuzzle.com/) allow you to turn videos into lessons by adding questions or links to related content. Tools like ThingLink (https://www.thinglink.com/) allow you to annotate images to take students on a journey through the material. There are many interactive options out there, and most are accessible, easily found and free to use.

- **Resource Bulletin Boards**: Websites like Pinterest (www.pinterest.com) and Padlet (https://padlet.com/), among many others, can be set up to allow students to add links to articles, websites, videos and other resources the find online related to whatever topic you propose. This has the added benefit of being a great way to build your own collection of resources to make available to future students.

- **Wrappers**: Metacognition is an important part of learning that involves having the students reflect on the learning process itself, and it deserves a mention here. An exam wrapper or lesson wrapper involves asking students to reflect on their learning behaviors, their confidence in their learning, their strengths and their needs.

7.3   Summative Assessments

The gold standard for summative assessment is a test or exam. However, is this the best tool to assess whether students have achieved the learning objectives you have for your course? For example, if your learning objective is to be able to apply the information learned to real life situations, will a multiple-choice exam let you know whether the students have mastered this skill? If your learning objective is to have students apply MLA style within a paper, can you do this in a test? Probably not. Luckily, modern learning management software allows for many summative assessment options that will let you know with certainty whether students have learned the information and skills you want them to have. Here are some options:

- **Exams**: If the material you teach is best assessed using an exam, then there are some important aspects to consider. Decide if proctors will be required and if the tests will be timed. Will they be "closed book and notes" and, if so, how will you make sure the students are not using their materials or other websites while they work? It's best to assume that reference material will be used unless you require proctoring. To maximize the effectiveness of an exam when you want to test more than a student's ability to use notes or websites, create a time limit. About one minute per question is a good benchmark for a multiple-choice, matching, or true-false question. Also, scramble the questions and/or answer choices so no two instances of the exam are the same. Finally, avoid using the textbook's question bank if possible. Websites such as Quizlet (https://quizlet.com/) are fantastic study tools for students, but a quick web search can turn up every question contained in a publisher's test bank within days of its release. Keep in mind that online automated grading is available only for objective exams, but essay and short answer exams are quite possible to set up.

- **Papers**: Students can submit papers, long or short, online. There are even anti-plagiarism tools to help save you time in helping students to avoid academic dishonesty. If your institution partners with Turnitin (https://www.turnitin.com/), make use of it. Many learning management systems have built-in plagiarism checkers, such as SafeAssign in BlackBoard and Moodle. Also, consider adding a peer review element to allow students to give feedback to each other before a final version is submitted for grading.
- **Group Projects**: Tools such as chat rooms, group discussion boards, wikis and document sharing make group projects a much more reasonable reality in online courses than they have ever been before. Don't hesitate to consider these, but keep in mind that students in online courses may have challenges when scheduling meeting times with their group members. They signed up for an asynchronous course unless your course description specifically calls for scheduled meetings, and they likely chose that format for a reason.

- **Presentations**: As with group projects, presentations are quite easy to assign in online courses. Students record themselves presenting or use a free screen capture application, such as Screen-Cast-O-Matic (https://screencast-o-matic.com/screen-recorder) to record themselves scrolling through a slide presentation with a voice-over. Many learning management systems have built-in video software and students can upload their videos to YouTube while controlling the privacy of the upload.

- **Case Studies**: Whether these are completed as interactive multimedia assignments, papers, or discussion forums, case studies have the ability to assess whether students can apply the information they are learning.

- **Portfolios**: There are many tools to help students to create portfolios, both within and outside of the standard learning management system applications. Students can submit their work as separate assignments throughout the semester or as a single capstone assignment toward the end of the course. Groups of students can work together using a wiki or shared document resource (such as Google Drive or Dropbox).

- **Podcasts**: Similar to presentations, podcasts are audio logs that students can create as either a single assignment or journal-style semester assignment.

- **Projects**: This is a broad category. If you have a project that you or a colleague used in a face-to-face course, it's likely that it can be adapted for online use. Consult with the distance learning and library resources available at your college for ideas to help you turn your project into an online-friendly assignment. For project ideas, explore the Internet or talk to the full-time faculty in your department.

Figure 5
FACULTY SELF-EVALUATION

Grade yourself from A to F on how well you perform in each of these areas in your online teaching.

TECHNOLOGY

I have all the necessary equipment to teach online. _____

I have all the necessary back-ups in place. _____

NAVIGATION

My course is easy to navigate. _____

I have posted information in multiple places. _____

ORGANIZATION

I have posted all information for my course before the

term begins. _____

I check into the course daily or almost daily. _____

COMMUNICATION

I respond to students in a timely fashion. _____

My interaction with students is always personal

and professional. _____

I have been able to create a caring community in my course. _____

PEDAGOGY

I use a variety of activities to appeal to different learning

styles. _____

ASSESSMENT

Assessment is varied and appropriate. _____

I give thoughtful feedback in a timely manner. _____

ACCESSIBILITY

I have checked my Web site for accessibility and made

recommended changes. _____

Figure 6
INTERPRETING COURSE EVALUATIONS

There are multiple opportunities to solicit student feedback throughout the semester. The feedback students provide about your teaching on their end-of-semester course evaluations is the most identifiable form of feedback and can be valuable in helping you improve and refine your teaching. Soliciting mid-semester student feedback has the additional benefit of allowing you to hear your students' concerns while there is still time in the semester to make appropriate changes. Adapted from "Some Guidelines and Principles to Consider In Making Sense of Evaluation Feedback," by Kathleen Hoover-Dempsey, Professor of Psychology, Emeritus, Vanderbilt University.

When considering student evaluations:

- Track quantitative results. Consider how the summary rating received for each item fits with your own teaching goals and your department's expectations for teaching.
- Look for patterns in students' comments—identify trends, note what you have done well and what needs improvement.
- Take your experience into account. If you are new to teaching, the school, or even the course, you may still be learning about various aspects of being a professor, such as course design, teaching skills, student interaction, and departmental expectations.

When dealing with negative student feedback:

- Know that almost all faculty members receive negative feedback at some point in their careers, including those who are senior and highly successful.
- Allow yourself to acknowledge that it can feel hurtful or make you angry, but also provides a pointer toward important areas for your continued development.
- When deciding how to further your development as a teacher:
- Bear in mind the most frequently mentioned areas for teaching improvement in analysis of student evaluations within and across universities: 1) clearer, more specific in-class communication; and 2) clearer, more explicit organization of course content.

RESOURCES

Journals

Stay current in the field by regularly reading the latest research and opinion pieces from experts. Here are some of the best journals and Web sites available:

American Center for the Study of Distance Education, maintained by Penn State's College of Education: https://sites.psu.edu/acde/

American Journal of Distance Education, abstracts of scholarly articles from the journal: https://www.tandfonline.com/loi/hajd20. Contact: The American Center for the Study of Distance Education, The Pennsylvania State University, College of Education, 303 Keller Building, University Park, PA 16802-3202.

Center for Research on Teaching and Learning, maintained by the University of Michigan, includes links to articles on teaching strategies, many related to distance education: http://www.crlt.umich.edu/

Chronicle of Higher Education: **Information Technology,** the education newspaper's IT section: https://www.chronicle.com/section/Technology/30/

Computers and Education: abstracts and scholarly articles from the journal. https://www.journals.elsevier.com/computers-and-education/

Distance Education: abstracts and scholarly articles from the journal. https://www.tandfonline.com/toc/cdie20/current

Distance-Educator.com, with reports available through the Distance EdeZine link: http://www.distance-educator.com/

Educational Technology, Research and Development, a journal of research on educational technology at all levels: https://aect.org/reference_library.php. Contact: Association for Educational Communications and Technology, 320 W. 8th Street, Ste. 101, Bloomington, IN 47404; 877-677-AECT or 812-335-7675

Institute for Learning Technologies, a list of projects under way in distance education: http://www.ilt.columbia.edu/

Instructional Technology Council, a site with links to research and awards related to distance education, as well as directories of learning object repositories and online courses: https://www.itcnetwork.org/

International Journal on E-Learning: abstracts and scholarly articles from the journal. http://www.aace.org/pubs/ijel/

Interpersonal Computing and Technology Journal, a peer-reviewed journal focused on computer-mediated communication in education: https://aect.org/reference_library.php. Contact: Association for Educational Communications and Technology, 1800 North Stonelake Drive, Suite 2, Bloomington, IN 47404; 812.335.7675.

Journal of Asynchronous Learning Networks focuses on research in online learning: https://onlinelearningconsortium.org/read/olc-online-learning-journal/. Contact: JALN, The Sloan Center at Olin and Babson Colleges, Franklin W. Olin College of Engineering, Olin Way, Needham, MA 02492-1200; 781-292-2523

Journal of Educators Online: abstracts and scholarly articles from the journal. https://www.thejeo.com/

Journal of Higher Education: abstracts and scholarly articles from the journal. https://muse.jhu.edu/journal/90

Journal of Interactive Online Learning, a peer-reviewed journal full of excellent research articles on distance education: http://www.ncolr.org/issues/index.html. Contact: JIOL, The University of Alabama, Tuscaloosa, AL 35487; 205-348-7010

Journal of Research on Technology in Education: abstracts and scholarly articles from the journal. https://www.iste.org/learn/edtech-research

Learning, Media, and Technology: abstracts and scholarly articles from the journal. https://www.tandfonline.com/toc/cjem20/current

T.H.E. Journal: Technological Horizons in Education, a magazine with a heavy emphasis on the technology: https://thejournal.com/Home.aspx Contact: 6300 Canoga Ave., Ste. 1150, Woodland Hills, CA 91367; 818-814-5277

Online Learning Journal: abstracts and scholarly articles from the journal. https://onlinelearningconsortium.org/read/olc-online-learning-journal/

Open Learning: The Journal of Open, Distance, and eLearning: abstracts and scholarly articles from the journal. https://www.tandfonline.com/toc/copl20/current

Quarterly Review of Distance Education: abstracts and scholarly articles from the journal. https://www.infoagepub.com/quarterly-review-of-distance-education.html

Technology, Pedagogy, and Education: abstracts and scholarly articles from the journal. https://www.tandfonline.com/toc/rtpe20/current

United States Distance Learning Association, with a link to archives of the *USDLA Journal*: https://usdla.org/

Websites/Professional Organizations

Professional organizations and websites dedicated to distance learning are excellent sources of the latest information to keep you up to date:

American Association for Adult and Continuing Education (AAACE), publications, conferences, and awards related to adult education: https://www.aaace.org/default.aspx

Association for the Advancement of Computing in Education (AACE): conferences, publications and resources: http://www.aace.org/

Blended Learning Toolkit: https://blended.online.ucf.edu/

Center for Research on Teaching and Learning: maintained by the University of Michigan, includes links to articles on teaching strategies, many related to distance education. http://www.crlt.umich.edu/

Chronicle of Higher Education: https://www.chronicle.com/

Consortium of College and University Media Centers (CCUMC): https://www.ccumc.org/default.aspx

Distance-Educator.com: http://www.distance-educator.com/

Educause: https://www.educause.edu/eli

Institute for Learning Technologies: http://www.ilt.columbia.edu/

Instructional Technology Council: http://www.itcnetwork.org/

International Council for Open and Distance Education: https://www.icde.org/

National Institute for Staff and Organizational Development (NI-SOD): https://www.nisod.org/

Online Learning Consortium, a site with many resources and awards: https://onlinelearningconsortium.org/

Society for Information Technology and Teacher Education (SITE): http://site.aace.org/

T.H.E. Journal: Technological Horizons in Education, a magazine with a heavy emphasis on the technology. http://www.thejournal.com/

United States Distance Learning Association: https://usdla.org/

WICHE Cooperative for Educational Technologies (WCET): https://wcet.wiche.edu/

Listservs and Other Discussion Forums

Sharing experiences and concerns is easy through online discussion forums, with listservs delivered through e-mail the most common structure. Here are some gatherings you may want to check out:

EDUCAUSE Community, *a series of discussion groups about information technology: https://www.educause.edu/community*

Web Based Training/Online Learning Listserv, focused on the development of Web-based training and e-learning programs: http://www.trainingplace.com/source/thelist.html

eLearning Blogs

From learning theories to content design, metadata to learning management systems, survey data to industry trends, these blogs have it all:

Adjunctnation.com, the "Teaching in Pajamas" blog is dedicated to distance learning, but all of their blogs are top notch: https://www.adjunctnation.com/category/nation-blogs/

Digital Chalkie: http://www.digitalchalkie.com/

Digital Writing, Digital Teaching: http://hickstro.org/

Edublogger, great set of blogs created by teachers with encouragement to use blogs as a teaching tool: https://www.theedublogger.com/

Elearningpost: http://www.elearningpost.com/

E-Learning Queen: http://elearnqueen.blogspot.com/

Emerging Ed-Tech, find out about the lasted ed-tech tools and resources: https://www.emergingedtech.com/

Khan Academy, excellent educational resource and blog to keep you up to date: https://www.khanacademy.org/about/blog

Online Learning Update: http://people.uis.edu/rschr1/onlinelearning/blogger.html

TED Ed, the repository of fantastic educational videos also has a blog. Visit for the blog but stay to explore the Ted Talk videos: http://blog.ed.ted.com/

The Rapid eLearning Blog: http://www.articulate.com/rapid-elearning/

Tony Karrer's eLearning Technology: http://elearningtech.blogspot.com/

Udemy, another excellent resource with a blog to keep you up to date: https://about.udemy.com/blog/

Conferences and Webinars

Here are some of the better known conferences related to distance education:

ADistance Teaching and Learning Conference (DT&L): annual conference focusing on distance education. https://dtlconference.wisc.edu/

Educause Annual Conference, information about the annual conference. Explore the site to find webinars and online conference events as well: https://events.educause.edu/annual-conference

eLearning Guild, several smaller conferences held throughout the year, as well as online events such as webinars: https://www.elearningguild.com/content.cfm?selection=doc.24

ISTE, annual conference and lots of useful resources. Be sure to explore the whole site: https://conference.iste.org

NISOD, annual conference, publications, and excellent webinars. Check to see if your college is a member institution for free resources and discounts: https://www.nisod.org/

Society for Information Technology and Teacher Education (SITE), annual conference and other resources: http://site.aace.org/conf/

Awards

The following awards in the area of distance education are open to adjunct instructors. Some come with cash awards; others offer recognition that can help advance your career:

Instructional Technology Council: Colleges are invited to submit nominations for awards in eLearning, with four awards given annually. Information: https://www.itcnetwork.org/itc-awards-excellence-elearning

MERLOT: Faculty can submit material for consideration for an award for "exemplary online learning resources" that includes $500 cash, a $1000 travel stipend, and free conference registration to MERLOT's annual international conference. Information: http://info.merlot.org/merlothelp/MERLOT_Awards_Exemplary_Classics.htm.

National Education Association: Three $2500 Excellence in the Academy awards (plus travel expenses to the annual convention) are given to full- or part-time faculty members each year for essays about teaching, which have included those about teaching online. Information: http://www2.nea.org/he/ajeaward.html.

Online Learning Consortium: Several different online teaching excellence awards. Information: https://onlinelearningconsortium.org/about/olc-awards/olc-awards-excellence-online-teaching-learning/

U.S. Distance Learning Association: This organization gives an annual award for Excellence in Distance Learning Teaching. Nomination is required, https://usdla.org/awards/

Figure 7 Sample Course Development Contract

XYZ University Course Development Contract

Faculty Member will receive $2000 to develop for XYZ University online course Math 110.

Training:
Faculty Member is required to attend faculty training sessions on any two of the following topics: Online Course Design, Managing Online Students, Using Online Communication Tools.

Deadlines:
A syllabus is due to the distance education coordinator by November 15, 2017. The finished course must be ready for evaluation by March 15, 2018. All revisions to the course must be completed by April 15, 2018. The course will be offered beginning in the 2006 summer semester.

Description:
The following are required elements of every online course at XYZ University:
Syllabus
Course objectives
Content modules
Detailed assignment descriptions
Lectures (one per module)
Plan for the use of discussion boards
Ownership:
XYZ University will hold copyright to all original course materials developed under this agreement, and no royalty or residual payments will be due to Annie Adjunct for the use of these materials.

Reviewed and approved by:

Faculty member signature:
Date:

Copyright Fair Use Guidelines for College Faculty

Courtesy of the Stanford Copyright and Fair Use Center, Stanford University Libraries, Stanford University, 2017 (http://fairuse.stanford.edu/).

What Types of Creative Work Does Copyright Protect?

Copyright protects works such as poetry, movies, CD-ROMs, video games, videos, plays, paintings, sheet music, recorded music performances, novels, software code, sculptures, photographs, choreography and architectural designs.

To qualify for copyright protection, a work must be "fixed in a tangible medium of expression." This means that the work must exist in some physical form for at least some period of time, no matter how brief. Virtually any form of expression will qualify as a tangible medium, including a computer's random access memory (RAM), the recording media that capture all radio and television broadcasts, and the scribbled notes on the back of an envelope that contain the basis for an impromptu speech.

In addition, the work must be original — that is, independently created by the author. It doesn't matter if an author's creation is similar to existing works, or even if it is arguably lacking in quality, ingenuity or aesthetic merit. So long as the author toils without copying from someone else, the results are protected by copyright.

Permission: What Is It and Why Do I Need It?

Obtaining copyright permission is the process of getting consent from a copyright owner to use the owner's creative material. Obtaining permission is often called "licensing"; when you have permission, you have a license to use the work. Permission is often (but not always) required because of intellectual property laws that protect creative works such as text, artwork, or music. If you use a copyrighted work without the appropriate permission, you may be violating—or "infringing"—the owner's rights to that work. Infringing someone else's copyright may subject you to legal action. As if going to court weren't bad enough, you could be forced to stop using the work or pay money damages to the copyright owner.

As noted above, permission is not always required. In some situations, you can reproduce a photograph, a song, or text without a license. Generally, this will be true if the work has fallen into the public domain, or if your use qualifies as what's called a "fair use." Both of these legal concepts involve quite specific rules. In most cases, however, permission is required, so it is important to never assume that it is okay to use a work without permission.

Many people operate illegally, either intentionally or through ignorance. They use other people's work and never seek consent. This may work well for those who fly under the radar—that is, if copyright owners never learn of the use, or don't care enough to take action.

Obtaining Clearance for Coursepacks

It is the instructor's obligation to obtain clearance for materials used in class. Instructors typically delegate this task to one of the following:

- Clearance services. These services are the easiest method of clearance and assembly.
- University bookstores or copy shops. University policies may require that the instructor delegate the task to the campus bookstore, copy shop, or to a special division of the university that specializes in clearances.

Using a Clearance Service

It can be time-consuming to seek and obtain permission for the 20, 30, or more articles you want to use in a coursepack. Fortunately, private clearance services will, for a fee, acquire permission and assemble coursepacks on your behalf. After the coursepacks are created and sold, the clearance service collects royalties and distributes the payments to the rights holders. Educational institutions may require that the instructor use a specific clearance service.

The largest copyright clearing service is the Copyright Clearance Center (www.copyright.com), which clears millions of works from thousands of publishers and authors.

Educational Uses of Non-Coursepack Materials

Unlike academic coursepacks, other copyrighted materials can be used without permission in certain educational circumstances under copyright law or as a fair use. "Fair use" is the right to use portions of copyrighted materials without permission for purposes of education, commentary or parody.

The Code of Best Practices in Fair Use for Media Literacy Education

In 2008, the Center for Media and Social Impact, in connection with American University, unveiled a guide of fair use practices for instructors in K–12 education, in higher education, in nonprofit organizations that offer programs for children and youth, and in adult education. The guide identifies five principles that represent acceptable practices for the fair use of copyrighted materials. You can learn more at the center's website, (www.cmsimpact.org).

Guidelines Establish a Minimum, Not a Maximum

In a case alleging 75 instances of infringement in an educational setting, 70 instances were not infringing because of fair use and for other reasons. The infringements were alleged because of the posting of copyrighted books within a university's e-reserve system. The court viewed the Copyright Office's 1976 Guidelines for Educational Fair Use as a minimum, not a maximum standard. The court then proposed its own fair use standard—10 percent of a book with less than ten chapters, or of a book that is not divided into chapters, or no more than one chapter or its equivalent in a book of more than ten chapters.—*Cambridge University Press v. Georgia State University*, Case 1:08-cv-01425-OD (N.D. Ga., May 11, 2012).

What is the Difference Between the Guidelines and Fair Use Principles?

The educational guidelines are similar to a treaty that has been adopted by copyright owners and academics. Under this arrangement, copyright owners will permit uses that are outlined in the guidelines. In other fair use situations, the only way to prove that a use is permitted is to submit the matter to court or arbitration. In other words, in order to avoid lawsuits, the various parties have agreed on what is permissible for educational uses, codified in these guidelines.

What is an "Educational Use?"

The educational fair use guidelines apply to material used in educational institutions and for educational purposes. Examples of "educational institutions" include K-12 schools, colleges, and universities. Libraries, museums, hospitals, and other nonprofit institutions also are considered educational institutions under most educational fair use guidelines when they engage in nonprofit instructional, research, or scholarly activities for educational purposes. "Educational Purposes" are:

- noncommercial instruction or curriculum-based teaching by educators to students at nonprofit educational institutions
- planned noncommercial study or investigation directed toward making a contribution to a field of knowledge, or
- presentation of research findings at noncommercial peer conferences, workshops, or seminars.

Rules for Reproducing Text Materials for Use in Class

The guidelines permit a teacher to make one copy of any of the following: a chapter from a book; an article from a periodical or newspaper; a short story, short essay, or short poem; a chart, graph, diagram, drawing, cartoon, or picture from a book, periodical, or newspaper.

Teachers may not photocopy workbooks, texts, standardized tests, or other materials that were created for educational use. The guidelines were not intended to allow teachers to usurp the profits of educational publishers. In other words, educational publishers do not consider it a fair use if the copying provides replacements or substitutes for the purchase of books, reprints, periodicals, tests, workbooks, anthologies, compilations, or collective works.

Rules for Reproducing Music

A music instructor can make copies of excerpts of sheet music or other printed works, provided that the excerpts do not constitute a "performable unit," such as a whole song, section, movement, or aria. In no case can more than 10 percent of the whole work be copied and the number of copies may not exceed one copy per pupil. Printed copies that have been purchased may be edited or simplified provided that the fundamental character of the work is not distorted or the lyrics altered.

A student may make a single recording of a performance of copyrighted music for evaluation or rehearsal purposes, and the educational institution or individual teacher may keep a copy. In addition, a single copy of a sound recording owned by an educational institution or an individual teacher (such as a tape, disc, or cassette) of copyrighted music may be made for the purpose of constructing aural exercises or examinations, and the educational institution or individual teacher can keep a copy.

Rules for Recording and Showing Television Programs

Nonprofit educational institutions can record television programs transmitted by network television and cable stations. The institution can keep the tape for 45 days, but can only use it for instructional purposes during the first ten of the 45 days. After the first ten days, the video recording can only be used for teacher evaluation purposes, to determine whether or not to include the broadcast program in the teaching curriculum. If the teacher wants to keep it within the curriculum, he or she must obtain permission from the copyright owner. The recording may be played once by each individual teacher in the course of related teaching activities in classrooms and similar places devoted to instruction (including formalized home instruction). The recorded program can be repeated once if necessary, although there are no standards for determining what is and is not necessary. After 45 days, the recording must be erased or destroyed.

A video recording of a broadcast can be made only at the request of and only used by individual teachers. A television show may not be regularly recorded in anticipation of requests—for example, a teacher cannot make a standing request to record each episode of a PBS series. Only enough copies may be reproduced from each recording to meet the needs of teachers, and the recordings may not be combined to create teaching compilations. All copies of a recording must include the copyright notice on the broadcast program as recorded and (as mentioned above) must be erased or destroyed after 45 days.

REFERENCES

8 astonishing Stats on Academic Cheating. (2019). Retrieved April 4, 2019, from https://oedb.org/ilibrarian/8-astonishing-stats-on-academic-cheating/

"A profile of participation in distance education: 1999-2000." National Center for Education Statistics. Retrieved November 9, 2004 from the World Wide Web: <http://nces.ed.gov/pubs2003/2003154.pdf>.

Adams, P., & Gingras, H. Blending Learning and Flipped Classrooms: A Comprehensive Guide (1st ed.). Ann Arbor: The Part-Time Press, 2018.

Angelo, T., & Cross, P. K. Classroom assessment techniques: A handbook for college teachers (2nd ed.). San Francisco: Jossey-Bass, 1993.

Baker, E. L. "Multiple Measures: Toward Tiered Systems." Educational Measurement Issues and Practices, Vol. 22, No. 2 (pp. 13-17), 2005.

Baker, Jason D. "An investigation of relationships among instructor immediacy and affective and cognitive learning in the online classroom." The Internet and Higher Education, vol. 7, no. 1 (Pages 1-13), (2004).

Bonk, C. J., Wisher, R. A., & Lee, J. "Moderating learner-centered e-learning problems and solutions, benefits and implications." In
T. S. Roberts (Ed.). Online collaborative learning: Theory and practice (pp. 54-85) . Hershey, Pa.: Idea Group, 2003.

Bramucci, R. (2001). "Ideas for distance learning." Retrieved September 11, 2004 from the World Wide Web: <http://fdc.ful-lerton.edu/learning/STG2001_IDEAS.htm>.

Burgstahler, S. (2017, January 30). ADA Compliance for Online Course Design. Retrieved January 20, 2018, from https://er.educause.edu/articles/2017/1/ada-compliance-for-online-course-design

Carter, Jarrett. "Study: Online Learning Improves Retention, Graduation Rates". Education Dive, 2018, https://www.educationdive.com/news/study-online-learning-improves-retention-graduation-rates/521271/.

Gardner, H. Multiple intelligences: The theory in practice. New York: Basic Books, 1993.

Greive, Donald. A Handbook for Adjunct/Part-Time Faculty and Teachers of Adults (6th ed.). Ann Arbor: Part-time Press, Inc, 2006.

Dekke, S., Lee, N. C., Howard-Jones, P., & Jolles, J. (2012). Neuromyths in education: Prevalence and predictors of misconceptions among teachers. Frontiers in Psychology, 3. doi: 10.3389/fpsyg.2012.00429.

Felder, Richard. "Understanding student differences." Journal of Engineering Education, January, 2005.

First Generation Students. (2018, August 1). Retrieved April 6, 2019, from http://pnpi.org/first-generation-students/

InsideHigherEd.com. "Survey of Faculty Attitudes on Technology," 2018.

James, Scott et al. "Retention, Progression And The Taking Of Online Courses". Online Learning, vol 20, no. 2, 2015. The Online Learning Consortium, doi:10.24059/olj.v20i2.780.

Lazarus, B.D. "Teaching courses online: How much time does it take?" Journal of asynchronous learning networks ,7(3) . Retrieved November 9, 2004 from the World Wide Web: <http://www.sloan-c.org/publications/jaln/v7n3/v7n3_lazarus.asp>.

Mayer, R.E. The promise of multimedia learning: using the same instructional design methods across different media. Learning and Instruction, vol. 13 no. 2 (Pages 125-139), 2003.

Merisotis, Jamie P. & Phipps, Ronald A. Institute for Higher Education Policy (2000). "Quality on the Line: Benchmarks for Success in Internet-Based Distance Education."

Moore, M. G., & Anderson, W. G. (Eds.). Handbook of distance education. Mahwah, N.J.: Lawrence Erlbaum, 2003.

Moser, S., & Smith, P. (2015). Benefits of Synchronous Online Courses. ASCUE Proceedings,43-48. Retrieved April 4, 2019, from the World Wide Web: <https://files.eric.ed.gov/fulltext/ED571270.pdf.>

Muilenburg, Lin, & Berge, Z. L. "A framework for designing questions for online learning." Retrieved September 2, 2004 from the World Wide Web: <http://www.emoderators.com/moderators/muilenburg.html>.

Neuhauser, C. "A maturity model: Does it provide a path for online course design?" Journal of interactive online learning, 3(1). Retrieved August 30, 2004 from the World Wide Web: <http:// www.ncolr.org/jiol/issues/>.

Opidee, I. (2015). Supporting first-gen college students. Retrieved from the World Wide Web: <https://www.universitybusiness.com/article/supporting-first-gen-college-students>.

Palloff, R. M., & Pratt, K. Building learning communities in cyberspace: Effective strategies for the online classroom. San Francisco: Jossey-Bass, 1999.

Palloff, R. M., & Pratt, K. The virtual student: A profile and guide to working with online learners. San Francisco: Jossey-Bass, 2003.

Parker, A. "Identifying predictors of academic persistence in distance education." USDLA Journal,17(1). Retrieved November 9, 2004 from the World Wide Web: <http://www.usdla.org/ html/journal/JAN03_Issue/article06.html>.

Postsecondary National Policy Institute. Factsheets: "First-Generation Students," September 26, 2018.

Prensky, M. Digital game-based learning. New York: McGraw-Hill, 2001.

"Quality on the line: Benchmarks for success in Internet-based distance education." The Institute for Higher Education Policy. Retrieved August 30, 2004 from the World Wide Web: <http://www.ihep.com/Pubs/PDF/Quality.pdf>.

Russell, T. L. The no significant difference phenomenon. Raleigh, N.C.: North Carolina State University, 1999.

Russell, Rich. "Don't Poke Me: Professors' Privacy in the Age of Facebook." AdjunctNation.com, November 1, 2010.

The Sloan Consortium. "Entering the mainstream: the quality and extent of online education in the United States, 2003 and 2004." Retrieved March 3, 2005 from the World Wide Web: http://www.sloan-c.org/resources/entering_mainstream.pdf.

The Sloan Consortium. "Sizing the opportunity: The quality and extent of online education in the United States, 2002 and 2003." Retrieved August 30, 2004 from the World Wide Web: <http://www.sloan-c.org/resources/sizing_opportunity.pdf>.

Spatariu, A., Hartley, K., & Bendixen, L. D. "Defining and measuring quality in online discussions." Journal of Interactive Online Learning, 2(4). Retrieved August 30, 2004 from the World Wide Web: http://www.ncolr.org/jiol/issues/showissue.cfm?volID=2&IssueID=9.

Starr, Linda. "The Educator's Guide To Copyright And Fair Use | Education World". Educationworld.Com, 2010, https://www.educationworld.com/a_curr/curr280.shtml.

Sunal, D. W., Sunal, C. S., Odell, M.R., & Sundberg, C. A. "Research-supported best practices for developing online learning." Journal of Interactive Online Learning, 2(1). Retrieved August 30, 2004 from the World Wide Web: <http://www.ncolr. org/jiol/issues/showissue.cfm?volID=2&IssueID=6>.

Van de Vord, Rebecca, & Korolyn Pogue. "Teaching time investment: Does online really take more time than face-to-face?." The International Review of Research in Open and Distributed Learning [Online], 13.3 (2012): 132-146. Web. 15 Jan. 2019

Wang, A. Y., & Newlin, M. H. "Online lectures: Benefits for the virtual classroom." T.H.E. Journal Online. Aug. 2001. Retrieved September 2, 2004 from the World Wide Web: <http:// www.the-journal.com/articles/15513>.

Wheeler, Gary S. Teaching and Learning in College (4th ed.). Ann Arbor: The Part-Time Press, Inc., 2003.

Willingham, Daniel T., et al. "The Scientific Status of Learning Styles Theories." Teaching of Psychology, vol. 42, no. 3, July 2015, pp. 266–271.

Ambrose, S., Bridges, M., Lovett, M., DiPietro, M., & Norman, M (2010). How Learning Works: 7 Research – Based Principles for Smart Teaching. San Francisco: Jossey-Bass.

Zimmerman, B. J. "Self-regulated learning and academic achievement: An overview." Educational Psychologist, 25 (1990): 3-17.

Index

Felder, Richard 54
fiber optic cable 12
field trips 7, 70
file transfer protocol. *See* FTP
formative assessment. *See* assessment
Form Builder 75
Fortner, Kelly 71
frequency 12
Frequently Asked Questions 25. *See* FAQ
FTP 12
full motion video 13
fully interactive video 13

G

Gamemaker 75
games 74. *See also* student interaction
Gardner, Howard 53
George Mason University 52
Georgia Perimeter College 70
Georgia State University 94
Gingras, H. 77, 97
Gmail 36
Google Docs 19
Google Drive 25, 82
Google Hangouts 36, 59, 68
Google Sheets 25
grades 17, 18, 28, 36, 43, 46, 59, 84
grading policy 43
group projects 81
Grunbaum, Suse 71
guest experts 69
Guidelines for Educational Fair Use 94

H

HDMI 13
Herreid, Clyde F. 73
High Definition Multimedia Interface. *See* HDMI
Holocaust Museum 71
Home Page 13. *See also* URL
host 13
Hot Potatoes 75
HTML 13
HTTP 13
Hypertext 13
Hyper Text Markup Language. *See* HTML
Hypertext Transfer Protocol. *See* HTTP

Savage, L.B. 65
Screen-Cast-O-Matic 82
self-regulated learners 28
Serial Line Internet Protocol. *See* SLIP
Skype 36, 68
Smith, P. 68
SoftChalk 79
spyware 17
Stanford University 92
State University of New York 73
St. Cloud State University 73
STEP508 55
storyboards 49
streaming audio. *See also* audio streaming
student conflicts 28
summative assessment 77. *See also* assessment
syllabus 16, 24, 25, 28, 30, 42, 44, 46, 49, 52, 71
Syllabus Finder 52
synchronous 37, 68

T

TCP 14
TEACH Act 50, 51
technology 9, 12, 17, 21, 22, 28, 32, 35, 45, 47, 48, 55, 57, 60,
74, 85, 86, 88
Technology, Education and Copyright Harmonization Act 50. *See* TEACH Act
TED 25
TED Talks 69
telecommunication 14
tests 22, 30, 31, 81, 95
The Sloan Consortium
ThingLink 80
threaded discussion. *See also* discussions
time management 22
Toptal 56
Transmission Control Protocol. *See* TCP
transponder 15
Turnitin 81
Turturice, Michael 71
Twitter 36

U

Understood 56
Uniform Resource Locator. *See* URL
Universal Course Design 48
Universal Design for Learning 56
University at Buffalo 73

New! The Power of Blended Learning in the Sciences

Take your science courses to the next level
- Design science courses that are fun to teach.
- Improve student learning outcomes.
- Spend less time lecturing and more time teaching.
- Learn to use blending to teach any type of science course or lab.

The Power of Blended Learning in the Sciences is a soup to nuts guide to everything you need to know about how to design courses in this format. The guiding theme of the book is that blended learning is not just another pedagogical fad, but rather an excellent framework for improving your teaching practice. While targeted for those who teach in the sciences, instructors in all disciplines will benefit from the accessible advice, well-structured format, and engaging writing. *The Power of Blended Learning in the Sciences* is available in paperback for $20.00.

New! Blended Learning & Flipped Classrooms: A Comprehensive Guide

Wish your students....

- Took responsibility for their learning?

- Completed coursework and actively participated in classroom discussions?

- Completed assigned work on time?

- Turned in assignments that followed directions/rubrics?

Flipped classrooms combined with blended learning strategies and techniques allow teaching faculty to combine their own creativity with technological tools that can make all of these "wishes" (and more) come true. Students in flipped and blended courses are more engaged, prepared and excited about the course materials you are eager to teach. Authors Patricia Adams and Happy Gingras—award-winning faculty members—have been teaching flipped and blended college courses for over a decade and in this book they take readers step-by-step through the process of flipping and blending a course. *Blended Learning & Flipped Classrooms* is available in paperback for $20.00.

Visit Part-TimePress.com

Part-Time Press, Inc. Instructional Products

Qty Total	Title	Unit $$
	Going the Distance, 2nd ed.	$15.00
	A Handbook for Adjunct/Part-Time Faculty, 7th ed.	$20.00
	Handbook II: Advanced Teaching Strategies, 4th ed.	$20.00
	Teaching Strategies and Techniques, 6th ed.	$15.00
	Excellent Online Science Teaching	$20.00
	Smile More. Grade Less. Cut Your Grading Time in Half.	$15.00
	Blended Learning and Flipped Classrooms	$20.00

BOOK PURCHASE SUBTOTAL:_____ add shipping _____

BOOK ORDER TOTAL:_____

☐ *Check (payable to The Part-Time Press)*
☐ *Credit Card #_____*
Exp. Date _____ CVV Code_____
☐ *Purchase Order #_____*

Name _____

Institution _____

Address _____

City/ST/Zip _____

Phone: _____

FAX: _____

E-mail: _____

Shipping and Handling Fee Schedule: *8% of purchase subtotal*
Send to: Part-Time Press, P.O. Box 130117, Ann Arbor, MI 48113-0117; Fax to: 734-665-9001; Phone 734-930-6854, or visit https://www.Part-TimePress.com